Walks with a point

The Ramblers' Association

DEVON

Walks with a point

Janice Anderson

Edited & revised by Bryan C. Linfoot

foulsham

London • New York • Toronto • Sydney

The Ramblers' Association
1-5 Wandsworth Road,
London SW8 2XX

Foulsham & Company Limited
Yeovil Road, Slough, Berkshire, SL1 4JH

The author wishes to thank Bryan Linfoot for his great help
in checking the details of the walks in this book.

ISBN 0-572-01758-8

Copyright 1992 Foulsham & Co. Ltd.

All rights reserved.
The Copyright Act (1956) prohibits (subject to certain very
limited exceptions) the making of copies of any copyright
work, including the making of copies by photocopying or
similar process.
Written permission to make a copy or copies must
therefore normally be obtained from the publisher in
advance. It is advisable also to consult the publisher if in
any doubt as to the legality of any copying which is to be
undertaken.

Please Note:
The publisher, author and the Ramblers' Association wish
to point out that whilst every effort has been made to
ensure accuracy, readers should note that changes in the
countryside take place all the time, and we cannot be held
responsible if details in the walk descriptions are found to
be inaccurate.

Where public rights of way are concerned, any obstacle or
hindrance should be reported to the Ramblers' Association
(see page 6) and the highway authority (see page 10).

Phototypeset in Great Britain by Typesetting Solutions, Slough, Berks.
Printed in Great Britain by Cox & Wyman Ltd, Reading, Berkshire.

The Ramblers' Association

The Ramblers' Association is a registered charity with three main aims.

- to protect footpaths and other rights of way and increase access to the open country.
- to defend outstanding landscapes.
- to encourage people to walk in the countryside.

It carries out these aims by running national campaigns, lobbying MPs, monitoring legislation, organising a national Family Rambling Day, and much more. At a local level, members help keep the footpath network open by walking paths regularly and by reporting path problems to highway authorities.

Since it was formed in 1935 the Ramblers' Association has grown steadily, and in 1992 membership topped 87,000. The Association's branch structure has also developed, in particular through the formation of local Groups which number over 330.

The threats to the countryside and its paths are growing. You can help us to deal with these threats simply by becoming a member, and walking with a local group if you wish. But there are also plenty of opportunities for joining in the practical footpath and amenity work carried out by your local Ramblers Group.

As a member you will be able to take advantage of the following benefits:

- **Rambling Today,** the Association's own quarterly magazine, plus your own area newsletter.
- Use of our 1:50,000 Ordnance Survey **Map Library.**
- **Discounts** in many outdoor equipment shops.
- Access to our national service of **expert advice and information.**

For an application form, write to Ramblers' Association, 1/5 Wandsworth Road, London SW8 2XX.

Protecting the Footpath Heritage

INTRODUCTION

The information given below is about the law relating to public paths (footpaths and bridleways) in England and Wales.

Public paths are highways in law. They have the same legal protection in principle as metalled carriageways, the difference being that paths are dedicated to use by limited classes of traffic, i.e. walkers on footpaths; and walkers, horse-riders and cyclists on bridleways.

An old legal maxim says 'once a highway always a highway'. This means that a public path can only be closed by a statutory procedure. It does not cease to be a public path simply because it is unused or little used.

HOW YOU CAN HELP

Paths are part of our heritage and need our protection. Every time you walk along a path you help to keep it open. By varying routes to include little known paths and by reporting any difficulties you meet you can make every step count in the struggle to preserve our country walks.

Reporting problems. Write to the relevant highway authority (see page 10) and tell the RA. The authority is the county council, metropolitan district council or London borough council. Give the location (six figure grid reference) and nature of problem, path number and name of owner or tenant (if known). However, if you are not very good at working out a grid reference, a written description with the nearest town, village or landmark will do. RA national office will supply you with problem report forms ready for use.

Obstructions. An obstruction is anything which hinders your free passage along a path, e.g. a barbed wire fence where there should be a gap or a stile. Highway authorities have a statutory duty to keep public paths open for public use and enjoyment.

Ploughing. If a path runs around the edge of a field its surface must not be ploughed or disturbed. If a path runs across a field, then the farmer is allowed to plough or disturb the surface when cultivating the land for a crop provided he could not conveniently avoid doing so and provided he restores the path surface within 24 hours of the disturbance (two weeks if the disturbance is the first one for a particular crop). A path so restored must be reasonably convenient to use, must have a minimum width of 1 metre for a footpath and 2 metres for a bridleway and its line must be clearly apparent on the ground. If this is not done the highway authority can, after giving notice to the farmer, go in, put matters right and send the bill to the farmer. It also has the power to take the farmer to court.

Crops. A farmer has a duty to prevent a crop (other than grass) from making the path difficult to find or follow. The minimum widths mentioned above apply here also, but if the path is a field-edge path they are increased to 1.5 metres for a footpath and 3 metres for a bridleway. You have every right to walk through crops growing on or over a path, but stick as close as you can to its correct line. Report the problem to the highway authority: it has power to prosecute the farmer or cut the crop and send him the bill.

Bridges and overgrowth. A missing bridge or overgrowth on the surface of the path are within the highway authority's maintenance responsibilities. Overgrowth from the sides of a path should be dealt with by the owner or tenant of the land. Again, the highway authority has power to act if he does not. (Note: Shire district councils are entitled to take over the maintenance of public paths from county councils if they wish and may by agreement take over other responsibilities from them).

Misleading notices. These are any signs which by false or misleading information may deter people from using a public path, are an offence on paths shown on the definitive map. Report to the highway authority.

Bulls. No bull over the age of ten months is allowed to be at large on its own in a field crossed by a public path, and no bull of a recognised dairy breed (Ayrshire, British Friesian, British Holstein, Dairy Shorthorn, Guernsey, Jersey and Kerry) is allowed in such a field under any circumstances. It is not a specific offence for beef or cross breed bulls to be at large in fields crossed by public paths if they are accompanied by cows or heifers, but if the bull endangers public safety an offence may be committed under Section 3 of the Health and Safety at Work Act 1974. Report any problems to the police.

PRACTICAL WORK

Increasingly, branches of the RA and local footpath and amenity societies are undertaking practical work to improve the condition of the paths.

This takes two main forms: path clearance and waymarking. Waymarking is carried out by painting arrows at points along the path where the route is unclear. Contact your local RA group if you would like to help.

FURTHER READING

Free leaflets on matters relating to rights of way in England and Wales produced by the RA are available from the RA office in London on receipt of an SAE. The RA also publishes, in conjunction with the Open Spaces Society, *Rights of Way: a Guide to Law and Practice*, a comprehensive book which includes the text of all relevant legislation.

LOCAL AUTHORITY

Footpaths Section, Devon County Council, Luccombe House, County Hall, Exeter, EX2 4QD. Telephone: Exeter (0392) 38200.

Contents

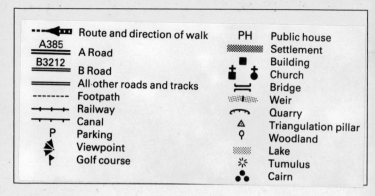

- - -◄▬▬ Route and direction of walk	**PH**	Public house
A385 A Road		Settlement
B3212 B Road	■	Building
All other roads and tracks	✝ ✝	Church
- - - - Footpath	⟑	Bridge
+ + + Railway		Weir
Canal	⌢	Quarry
P Parking	△	Triangulation pillar
Viewpoint	○	Woodland
Golf course		Lake
	⁕	Tumulus
	●●●	Cairn

The maps

The sketch maps in this book are meant to be used in conjunction with the Ordnance Survey Landranger and Pathfinder maps mentioned at the beginning of each walk. Symbols on the maps have been simplified and are meant to give rough guidance to the location of the symbols on the maps.

LOCATION OF WALKS

Major Roads

Motorways

Lorna Doone Country

Oare Common — Malmsmead Hill

MAP:	Ordnance Survey 'Landranger' Sheet 180; 'Pathfinder' No. 1214 (SS 64/74).
DISTANCE:	Nearly 7 miles (Malmsmead to Doone Valley and return is about 5 miles).
ROUGH GUIDE TO TIME TAKEN:	3½ - 4 hours (about 2½ for shorter walk).
TERRAIN:	Partly wooded valley with a stony or rocky surface, partly high moorland with a peaty surface. The first section is very popular in summer, the second less so, both are clearly marked.
FOOD AND DRINK:	Refreshments at Malmsmead and Cloud Farm (not winter time).
TRANSPORT:	Public car park (with a courtesy box for its use).
FACILITIES:	Toilets near public car park in Malmsmead.
START AND FINISH:	Malmsmead (reached by a turning off the A39 near County Gate between Lynmouth and Minehead) Grid reference: 792478.

WALK 1

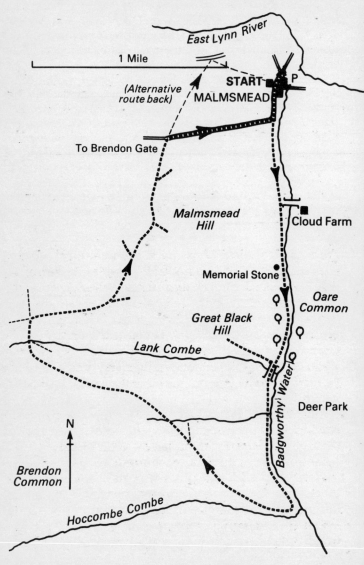

East Lynn River

1 Mile

(Alternative route back)

START
MALMSMEAD

P

To Brendon Gate

Malmsmead Hill

Cloud Farm

Memorial Stone

Oare Common

Great Black Hill

Lank Combe

Badgworthy Water

Deer Park

N

Brendon Common

Hoccombe Combe

Lorna Doone, the most famous of R. D. Blackmore's novels, is set on Exmoor, at the easternmost edge of Devon. Here, in 'a deep green valley, carved from the mountains in a perfect oval, with a sheer fence of rock around it', which was how he described Hoccombe Combe where it runs into Badgworthy Water, Blackmore set the settlement of fourteen cots where lived the notorious, murderous Doones.

Blackmore's tale was pure fiction, though it was based on stories, part fact and mostly legend, which had circulated in Devon for generations about a gang of robbers and murderers who had terrorised Exmoor in the 17th century. At this period, Exmoor was a wild place. There were no well-built roads linking neatly fenced farms; instead, a barren wilderness overgrown with heather made excellent territory for villains to go to ground in.

Today, as anyone following this walk will discover, the countryside of the Doones, though still wild and lonely, is no longer a place of terror.

From the Malmsmead car park, the walk turns left and goes towards Lorna Doone Riding Stables. Ignoring the path signposted 'Short cut to Doone Valley', keep to the right of the stables, carry on up the road a short distance to a gate indicated by a yellow waymark and a sign 'Public bridleway to Doone Valley'. Through the gate, the clearly defined path drops down again towards Badgworthy Water, keeping a little inland of the river, until it joins the 'Short Cut' path, ignored at the outset of the walk, near Cloud Farm.

After Cloud Farm, which is on the opposite bank and reached by a bridge, is passed, the rock strewn path is through very sparse woodland for a short distance until it comes out on to open, level ground.

Here you will see the memorial stone to R. D. Blackmore, the man who ensured the walk — or at least this section of it — its enormous summertime popularity.

Past the memorial stone, you once again walk into woodland, where you may spot a large variety of birds;

along the water, birds to watch out for include the dipper, grey wagtail and redstart. The land on the far (left-hand) bank of Badgworthy Water is Oare Common, and to the right and ahead rises Great Black Hill. At Yealcombe Water, flowing down into Badgworthy Water, on one's right is a gate to be negotiated, then the walk carries on through woodland, which becomes denser as one penetrates it; soon the Lank Combe stream can be seen flowing through coniferous woods on the far bank and in to Badgworthy Water.

After a short distance, the path crosses an open area then goes into the woods again to reach the footbridge over the Lank Combe stream coming down the side of Black Hill, through the woods and into Badgworthy Water.

Lorna Doone fans wanting to see the inspiration for Blackmore's 'Water Slide' — three slabs of stepped rocks which the water slips over — can make a short detour here by turning right and walking 20 yards or so up Lank Combe.

To continue with the walk, cross the footbridge and follow the path through the rocky area of Withycombe Ridge Water to reach a junction of paths. Take the path which turns right and goes up Hoccombe Valley for half a mile to Brendon Common.

This is the valley of the Doones, where there is enough evidence of habitation — a ruined cottage, overgrown boundaries outlining former fields, and a widening of the path itself — to indicate that people certainly lived here at one time; perhaps the Doones themselves?

(The walk thus far has taken about one and a quarter hours and covered some two and a half miles. It is a good enough introduction to Doone territory for those not wanting too long a walk to turn back here and retrace their steps to Malmsmead).

Continuing with the longer, circular route, you should

follow the track, which is a bridleway, on up the Hoccombe Valley and so up towards Withycombe Ridge. The path is reasonably distinct for the whole of this section, climbs steadily through wind-swept bracken and heather (gloriously purple in early autumn), crosses a stream and passes through a gate in a post and wire fence at what is about the highest point on this walk — about 1,200 feet above sea level — before contouring round Withycombe Ridge then down the valley side to cross Lank Combe again.

Over the far side of the Combe, climb up the opposite slope, at whose summit is a signpost: the right-hand route for this walk is the way signposted 'Malmsmead 2m'. As one crosses the open moor and ignoring all side paths, splendid views of the Bristol Channel and the coast of Wales beyond are seen on a fine day. The track then slopes down to cross a stream and then up again across the slope of Malmsmead Hill to reveal a more restricted view of the sea.

Soon the track comes to a metalled road. Turn right here to follow the road downhill, over a cattle grid, and so back to Malmsmead. (If you wish to avoid the road, you may cross over it, go through the gate here, and turn right to take the field path back to Malmsmead.)

Galsworthy's Manaton and the Hound of the Baskervilles

Wingstone — Swallerton Gate — Hound Tor

MAP:	Ordnance Survey 'Landranger' sheet 191; 'Pathfinder' Nos. 1328 (SX 68/78) and 1341 (SX 76/77).
DISTANCE:	About 6½ miles.
ROUGH GUIDE TO TIME TAKEN:	3½ hours.
TERRAIN:	Moderately easy walk, mostly over rolling moorland, though with steep gradients in places.
FOOD AND DRINK:	Pub and general store in Manaton.
TRANSPORT:	Car park below St Winifred's Church, north side Manaton (just off the B3344). A courtesy box is put here for the use of the park, the money helps the parish to maintain the car park.
FACILITIES:	No toilets anywhere near the walk.
START AND FINISH:	Car park (as above). Grid reference 750812.

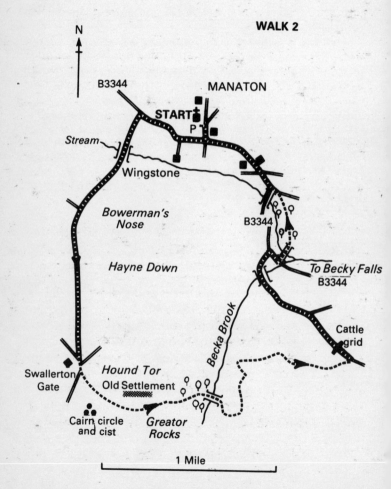

WALK 2

N

B3344

MANATON

START

P

Stream

Wingstone

Bowerman's Nose

B3344

Hayne Down

To Becky Falls
B3344

Becka Brook

Cattle grid

Swallerton Gate

Hound Tor
Old Settlement

Cairn circle and cist

Greator Rocks

1 Mile

Manaton is a delightfully unspoilt Dartmoor village with a pretty green, edged by an avenue of trees, and a church, St Winifred's, which contains fine stained glass dating from the 15th century. John Galsworthy, the Nobel Prize-winning author, although born in Surrey, was of a Devonshire family and discovered Wingstone Farm on the edge of Manaton during a walking tour. He honeymooned there in 1904, and spent most of his summers there from 1906, when *A Man of Property*, the first book in *The Forsyte Saga* sequence, was published, until 1923.

South of Manaton is magnificent moorland country, notable for its tors and rocky outcrops, including Bowerman's Nose, a stack of granite slabs with a distinctive 'nose' profile which takes its name from a man turned to stone by local witches, and the jagged Hound Tor. This tor was the one which Sir Arthur Conan Doyle provided with a phantom hound from Hell in *The Hound of the Baskervilles*. The hound killed bad Sir Hugo Baskerville, for whom Conan Doyle got his inspiration from Sir Richard Cabell of Brooke Manor, an evil man who died in 1677. Black dogs (hell-hounds?) were said to have come racing in from the moors to howl at his corpse in Buckfastleigh Church.

Outside the car park the walk turns right, then right again on to the narrow B3344. After about 300 yards, a tree-lined drive leaves the road to the left, leading to Wingstone, Galsworthy's house.

The walk continues another ¼ mile along the B3344 and takes the next turning on the left, a deep, narrow lane following the lane down the hill, across a small stream and passing through a gate on to the moor. The road now unfenced, climbs steeply up and around Bowerman's Nose. The views opening up behind are very fine. As Bowerman's Nose is passed on the left, the gradient eases and suddenly the rugged profile of Hound Tor appears against the skyline.

The walk now passes through another gate, called 'Moyles Gate' and continues along the road; a view across to Black Hill opens up on your left, with Hound Tor still dominating the view ahead.

At the end of the lane, you turn left opposite a very pretty thatch and stone cottage; a few yards further on is Swallerton Gate, a road junction and a car park. You continue in the same direction by leaving the road and striking out across the moor, climbing gently upwards and keeping Hound Tor about 75 yards to the left. As you climb steadily upwards you will see a group of isolated stones on the horizon, make for these. This is a cairn circle and a cist (stone coffin). Continue upwards but slightly to your left as if making for the majestic Haytor now in view. Soon you will come across a broad grassy track cutting across your path, turn left along this path which gently falls down the slope of the valley between Hound Tor and Greator Rocks. As you come down the slope you will pass through a gap in a wall and will see the remains of an abandoned village. This is a large site and one can spend much time examining the remains and wondering how such a sizable community could ever have existed in such a remote place.

Returning to the path, a short climb brings you up to a gate amongst the rocks on the skyline. A sign here directs you downhill towards Leighon via Haytor Down. Follow this path all the way down to Becka Brook through a series of gates and past the edge of a forest on the left. At the bottom of the valley, the path crosses Becka Brook by a bridge of stone slabs.

Now the path passes between rocks and steadily climbs up through low scrub and woodland, finally emerging once again on to the open moor. Here the walk turns left at the sign confirming the bridlepath and follows this through bracken and gorse (called furze in this part of the country) along the edge of Haytor Down. You pass into a clump of trees and a gate leading into an old sunken green lane. Note the fine views on the left back to Hound Tor and across to Hayne Down and Bowerman's Nose.

Once through the gateway, the path follows the sunken lane, passes through another gate, and rounds the corner to an old driveway down to Leighon House. Turn right here and climb the hill, go through another gate, then continue to climb steeply up through the bracken. Soon the path becomes a stony track, the gradient eases, and superb views open up on the left, back towards Manaton, the walk follows the track which crosses open moorland before joining the road, at which point there are further fine views ahead.

At the road, the walk turns left and off the moor across a cattle grid. As the road goes downward, the gradient becomes very steep in places and the lane is buried between characteristically steep Devon banks. At the bottom of the hill, the road crosses Becka Brook once again, and soon rejoins the B3344. You turn right here; 150 yards further on is the car park for Becky Falls which may be visited, after paying a suitable fee, by following the well-marked route much frequented by visitors. If the weather has been dry for some time, the falls will probably not be much more than a trickle.

Returning to the B3344, you retrace your steps a short distance, then, just across the bridge over the brook, there is a footpath on the right leading into a wood which you follow. However, there are many crossing tracks here and a forest walk that can be misleading. At the beginning turn left and follow a blue waymarked route until a crossing of tracks is reached, then turn left. If you are in doubt, always keep the little tumbling stream immediately on your left. Eventually you will emerge from the woods after crossing two stiles, then across a field to a gate and stile which leads back onto the road. Turn right and follow the B3344 back to Manaton and the car park.

Jane Austen
and Dickens at Dawlish

Dawlish Water — Gatehouse Hill — Brunswick Place

MAP:	Ordnance Survey 'Landranger' sheet 192; 'Pathfinder' No. 1342 (SX 87/97).
DISTANCE:	About 5¼ miles.
ROUGH GUIDE TO TIME TAKEN:	3 hours.
TERRAIN:	Moderately easy walking, with some steep sections in river valley and hill country above Dawlish.
FOOD AND DRINK:	Cafés and pubs in Dawlish.
TRANSPORT:	Pay and Display car park beside Dawlish Museum accessed from the town centre by taking one-way street (Brunswick Place) from roundabout on S. side of town.
FACILITIES:	At The Lawn 150 yards from car park (follow direction arrows).
START AND FINISH:	By Dawlish Museum (open daily May–September). Grid reference 958768.

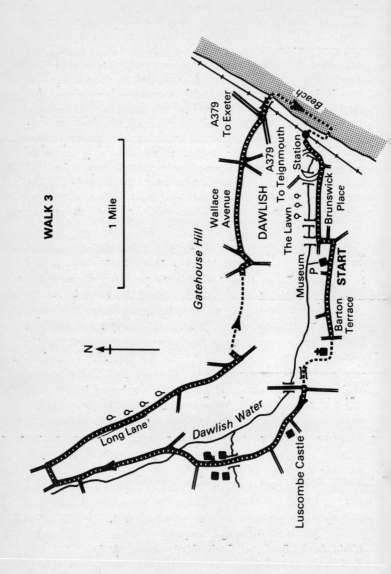

WALK 3

1 Mile

N

Beach

A379
To Exeter

Gatehouse Hill

Wallace Avenue

DAWLISH

A379
To Teignmouth

Station

The Lawn

Brunswick Place

Museum

P

START

Barton Terrace

Long Lane

Dawlish Water

Luscombe Castle

28

Described in a recent guide book as 'a sedate watering place' — a description in keeping with the style of Jane Austen, who liked the place very much — Dawlish was a fishing village which was turned into a seaside resort town late in the 18th century. Jane Austen, holidaying here in 1802, would have seen the beginning of the building work which resulted in The Lawn, now a lovely park, which was laid out beside Dawlish Water the following year, and the elegant row of Regency villas which still characterise the old part of Dawlish. Certainly she was charmed enough with the place to make Robert Ferrars say to Elinor Dashwood in *Sense and Sensibility* that it seemed rather surprising to him that anyone could live in Devonshire, without living near Dawlish.

Charles Dickens also found Dawlish an attractive place, and chose to make it — or at least a farm nearby — the birthplace of one of his more attractive heroes, Nicholas Nickleby.

From the car park beside Dawlish Museum in Barton Terrace the walk turns right into Barton Terrace. At the far end of the road, keep straight ahead into the churchyard; keep to the right round the far end, going out through the lich-gate into an open grassy area. Here the walk turns left along the path, through a gate, across a stream and out on to the road. Go straight ahead at this road junction, keeping well in to the right hand side of the road, and noting to the left the castellated bridge over the lane which carries one of the drives of Luscombe Castle, a mansion (not open to the public) built in 1800-4 by John Nash for the banker, Charles Hoare. On the left is a picturesque cottage and the boundary of the castle grounds. Soon, the lodge, and the grounds of the castle are passed, and, beyond them, the fine firs, cedars and pines of the Park can be seen. After a climb, the walk turns right at the road junction, passed a row of thatched cottages.

The gently undulating lane leads past Combe Brooke, a fine Victorian house and farm outbuildings and on to Lower Rixdale Farm, a large, rambling farmhouse. Here the road veers right and crosses Dawlish Water by means of a ford or footbridge.

At the next junction, the walk turns left and follows the road along a gentle valley past several cottages, one of which has unusual oak shingles; beyond, the horizon is topped by the pine woods of Great Haldon. After easy walking of about three-quarters of a mile, when you can see the group of greenhouses, take the road on the right which climbs steeply up out of the valley. At the top, having admired the extensive views over the Exe estuary, you turn right along Long Lane.

Shortly, the metalled road becomes a track and climbs gently along the ridge of hills above Dawlish Water. The view on the left now embraces the whole Exe estuary and the low red outcrops of Straight Point on the far side. The track levels out and passes beside a stretch of woodland; there is not much to see for a while, then there is a sudden view on the left across to Exmouth. Soon the road becomes metalled once more and drops down to a road junction, where you turn right.

After about 150 yards there is an opening between the gardens of two houses and a track on the left. A gate and stile give access to an open field. Keeping to the right-hand side of the field, ignore the stile in the corner but walk up to the stile giving access to the next field, cross the latter and go through another field with extensive views to the left. Across a third stile is the summit of the walk, crowned by a ring of lofty pines — there used to be six but the gales at the start of 1990 decimated them. The view is wonderful: to the left is the Exe estuary and the Dorset coast beyond, ahead is the open sea, towards the right is the Devon coast stretching away to Tor Bay, and immediately below on the right is Dawlish. The early 19th century kernel of the town sits in the valley of Dawlish Water, while the ranks of modern bungalows spread up the hillsides. At the head of the town is the parish church near where the walk began. Behind, the view extends to the forests of Great Haldon.

The walk continues on down the hill from the pines, alongside the hedge, then crosses a stile into a narrow tunnel-like path. Passing a range of greenhouses on the right, the path emerges on to Gatehouse Hill. Here you turn left, then immediately right into Wallace Avenue. Follow this road down hill, past distinctly non-Dickensian bungalows: about halfway down is seen Strand Hill which drops away on the right towards the town, between sheer walls of sandstone but ignore this and continue down the road. By now, the houses are getting older and larger — distinguished stuccoed villas.

Finally, modern blocks of holiday flats stand on the corner of the main A379 road. Here the walk turns left, crosses the pedestrian crossing, goes a few yards back to the right and passes through a gap in the wall and down a steep path to a footbridge over the railway line at the London end of Dawlish Station, built by Brunel to accommodate his railway line which had reached the town in 1846.

At the foot of the steps, you turn right either along the sea-wall or, if the tide permits, along the beach. At the far end of the station platform, built out on struts above the sand, turn right under the low railway bridge. Notice also that this is where Dawlish Water issues into the sea. Now you make your way across the roundabout and roads on to The Lawn, the central park flanking the banks of the stream, and walk up the left-hand side of The Lawn along Brunswick Place; at the top end of the road, turn left away from the stream and follow the road round into Barton Terrace to return to the museum and car park.

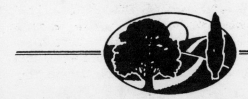

Rudyard Kipling at Rock House, Maidencombe

Watcombe — Maidencombe — the South Devon Coast Path

MAP:	Ordnance Survey 'Landranger' sheet 202; 'Pathfinder' No. 1351 (SX 86/96)
DISTANCE:	About 4¼ miles.
ROUGH GUIDE TO TIME TAKEN:	2¾ hours.
TERRAIN:	A coastal walk, sometimes steep or on precipitous cliff-tops, on an often rough track, with some road walking. Shoes or boots with a good grip on the soles are recommended.
FOOD AND DRINK:	Seasonal tea-room in Maidencombe, or carry a picnic.
TRANSPORT:	Car park at Watcombe, signposted off the A379 Teignmouth — Torquay Road.
FACILITIES:	Toilets down hill from car park near beach or at Maidencombe.
START AND FINISH:	Car park (as above). Grid reference 923675.

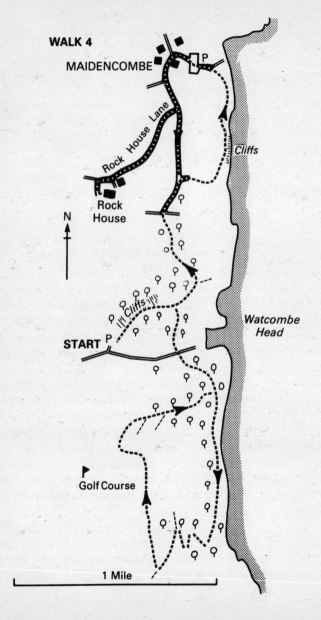

WALK 4

MAIDENCOMBE

Rock House Lane

Rock House

N

Cliffs

Cliffs

Watcombe Head

START P

Golf Course

1 Mile

Maidencombe, the mid-point of this circular walk along the South Devon Coast path, is a district overlooking Babbacombe Bay, north of Torquay. Here, in 1896, Rudyard Kipling and his wife Caroline discovered what seemed to them the perfect place — Rock House, down Rock House Lane — where the sunny aspect and the sea would surely supply the perfect atmosphere for writing. Less than a year later, they fled from the house, driven out by the 'spirit of deep, deep Despondency' which Kipling said overhung the house and which had caused a dreadful depression in them both. Despite this strange manifestation of the apparently paranormal, Kipling managed to begin several books at Rock House, including some 'parables on the education of the young' which turned into the splendidly lively *Stalky and Co.*, published in 1899.

The walk leaves the car park by a stile in the bottom corner, clearly marked for the 'Coast Walk to Labrador', a bit further than the one we are walking. The path runs down the side of a wooded gully, with sheer cliffs rising to the left. After a couple of hundred yards, a path branches off to the right — to which we will return later — and is signed 'Coast Path' in both directions, but for the moment the walk keeps straight ahead. Whilst we are on the Coast Path always follow these signs, as, from time to time, coastal erosion takes place and the path is then diverted to a safer route. Soon the path begins to rise, and suddenly there is a fine view of the sea. The path climbs the side of the cliffs by steep, badly worn steps; there is a handrail to help but this is on the inside of the path — there is nothing between the walkers and a sheer drop except a few low shrubs, so take extreme care! At the top of the climb is a bench on a precipitous outcrop from which to admire the view, then the path turns north and downwards along a wooded valley and back into woodland. Towards the bottom there is another fine view out to sea, then the path becomes a rough track and turns upward once more. At the top of the rise, there is another junction of paths — to which we will, again, later return

— but this time the walk turns right still following the Coast Path. The path heads down towards the cliff edge, then turns along the cliff, skirting a field. The walk follows the path on its switchback route along the cliff top, at times on the edge of a dizzy drop, at other times separated from the brink by trees and scrub.

Ahead you should now see Maidencombe, and before long the path emerges on to the narrow metalled road down to Maidencombe beach, opposite are some public conveniences. You should turn up this road skirting the car park, and into Maidencombe itself, where we leave the Coast Path. At the road junction, opposite the aptly named 'The Thatched Tavern', the walk turns left into Rock House Lane, past the houses and an hotel, then at the next junction marked Brim Hill it continues uphill.

This lane climbs very steeply upwards, turns shortly to the right and continues upwards for about a quarter of a mile. At the top on the left is Rock House, its name clearly marked on the large castellated gate posts. Across the road from the gates of the house is a very fine view north-eastwards across the Teign estuary and, beyond that, the mouth of the Exe and the Dorset coastline.

From Rock House, the walk retraces its way back down Rock House Lane to the point where it turns sharply to the left, you turn right on to a rough track marked 'No Through Road'. This path climbs gently up along the side of the hill, the gateway on the left offering fine views out to sea. Shortly the walk meets the junction of paths already visited, and back on to the Coast Path where it continues straight ahead to retrace the path all the way back down the cliff path to the first junction.

This time, the walk turns to the left along the Coast Path and follows a path through woodland, at one point dropping steeply down a flight of rough steps. Eventually this path emerges on to the road down to Watcombe beach. Here you turn left, then shortly right, back into the woods. The path climbs very steeply upwards by means of winding steps until the summit is reached, then becomes a broad walk dropping gently down through the trees, giving occasional views of the red cliffs of Watcombe Head breaking away into the sea. Another flight of steps leads up to another junction of paths to which, once again, we will return later.

Now the walk bears to the left and downwards, then southwards along the cliff edge. Ahead is a fine view of the coast towards Torquay and beyond. The switchback course of the path ends when it abruptly turns inland and climbs steeply by a series of dog-legs to join another path running along the hillside. Here, you turn left and, after 200 yards, emerge from the wood at an oblique junction of paths where there is a wide view of the Torquay suburbs of St Marychurch and Babbacombe. Here we leave the Coast Path and the walk turns sharply up to the right, passes through a hedge and out into a high open field, where it passes through another hedge. A few yards further on is a seat commanding the finest views of the whole walk from a height of some 125 metres (about 400 feet).

The path leaves the field and turns to the left, continuing to skirt the edge of the golf course, then to the right, and down into the lowermost corner of the field to find a stile in the hedge space, on to a path that heads downwards once more towards the sea. Ignoring all paths to the right, after several flights of steps through a wood, the path rejoins our original path. From there, you retrace the walk down the steep steps to the Watcombe beach road; turn left up the steep lane and shortly you will arrive at the car park on the right, and the end of the walk.

Shelley and the Valley of the Rocks

Lynton — Lynmouth

MAP:	Ordnance Survey 'Landranger' sheet 180; 'Pathfinder' No. 1214 (SX 64/74).
DISTANCE:	About 4¼ miles.
ROUGH GUIDE TO TIME TAKEN:	2¾ hours.
TERRAIN:	Moderately easy cliff-top and hill walking, a little steep in places.
FOOD AND DRINK:	Numerous cafés, tearooms in Lynton and Lynmouth.
TRANSPORT:	Pay and Display car parks (signposted in Lynton).
FACILITIES:	Toilets in public car park near Castle Hotel.
START AND FINISH	Lynton town centre, near the Valley of the Rocks Hotel. Grid reference 720496.

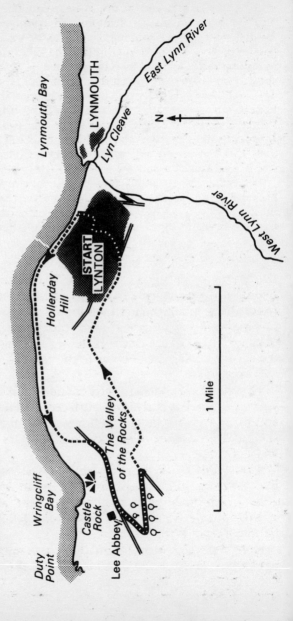

WALK 5

East Lynn River

West Lynn River

N

LYNMOUTH

Lynmouth Bay

Lyn Cleave

START
LYNTON

Hollerday Hill

The Valley
of the Rocks

Wringcliff Bay

Castle Rock

Lee Abbey

Duty Point

1 Mile

The Valley of the Rocks, marked by rock pinnacles weathered into bizarre shapes and forms, is near enough to the twin North Devon towns of Lynton and Lynmouth for its formations to be seen topping the hills to the west of them. A good road goes from Lynton direct to the Valley of the Rocks, but the most memorable way to reach it is to take the spectacular coast path, called the North Walk, from Lynton. This walk was the preferred way of the poet Shelley, who honeymooned in Lynmouth with his young bride, Harriet Westbrooke, in 1812. The couple spent over two months in Lynmouth (in a cottage which, although rebuilt after a fire early this century, is still called Shelley's Cottage), during which time Shelley wrote *Queen Mab*.

The walk here probably also helped inspire Coleridge's *Ancient Mariner*, for Dorothy Wordsworth recorded how her brother, William, and Coleridge discussed the ballad, which was to become the great poem, while walking here.

Among the several ways to the North Walk from Lynton/Lynmouth (including the famous 1890 cliff railway from Lynmouth), perhaps the easiest to find is the signposted route off the main street in Lynton. This is a narrow road turning down towards the coast by the right-hand side of the large Valley of the Rocks Hotel. Follow this way, past the church, and you will come to the coast path near the cliff railway.

The North Walk was properly cut out and laid over 150 years ago, and is a fairly level, surfaced path which twists and turns around the cliff 500 feet above the sea, with spectacular views of the rocky coast and across to the Welsh Coast.

After nearly a mile the cliff path, on which you will very likely have encountered some of the large and handsome goats which graze here, reaches open land and greensward, with the Valley of the Rocks on the left and the famous Castle Rock immediately ahead.

Here, the walk curves left and then turns right on to the road which goes up the valley to the left of Castle Rock towards Lee Abbey. (There is a path up Castle Rock for those wanting a fairly adventurous detour.) You should follow the sign-posted 'Coast Path' here, ignoring the private path to Wringcliff Bay. On the way up the valley to Lee Abbey the walk passes the beginning of a track which goes uphill to the left to Mother Meldrum's Cave, which featured in R. D. Blackmore's Lorna Doone. Jan Ridd came here to ask the old woman for advice in carrying on his love affair with Lorna.

Once at the Abbey (which was never an Abbey but a Victorian mansion — now one of the biggest mixed religious communities in Europe) the walk turns left through the gate opposite the arched entrance to the Abbey. This track, signposted 'Lynton over South Cliff', zig-zags uphill; at the second bend continue straight on through woodland about half-way up the hill.

After 100 yards or so, the path emerges from the wood and steadily but slowly climbs the bracken-covered hill, passes through a gate in a post-and-wire fence and continues to a high point where extensive views of the town and the bay can be seen on a clear day. The path then slowly descends towards Lynton, two miles from Lee Abbey.

Once above Lynton, there are several ways off the path and down to the town, and where you choose to come down will probably depend on where you parked the car. The way down back to the centre of the town is via Lydiate Lane.

A Walk to Bolt Head

Sharpitor — Bolt Head

MAP:	Ordnance Survey 'Landranger' sheet 202; 'Pathfinder' No. SX 63/73/83.
DISTANCE:	About 4¼ miles.
ROUGH GUIDE TO TIME TAKEN:	2½ — 2¾ hours.
TERRAIN:	Cliff-top and hilly farmland walking, steep in places.
FOOD AND DRINK:	Refreshments at Overbeck Garden and Museum; three hotels in South Sands.
TRANSPORT:	Car park at Overbeck Gardens, Sharpitor. Note in holiday season it is unwise to take the direct route from Malborough.
FACILITIES:	Toilets in Overbeck Gardens, after paying the parking fee, or nearer to Salcombe.
START AND FINISH:	Sharpitor. Grid reference 729375.

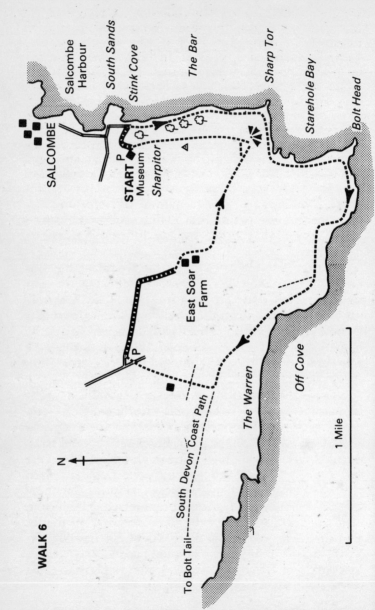

WALK 6

SALCOMBE

Salcombe Harbour
South Sands
Stink Cove
The Bar
Sharp Tor
Starehole Bay
Bolt Head

START
P
Museum
Sharpitor

East Soar Farm

P

The Warren

Off Cove

To Bolt Tail

South Devon Coast Path

N

1 Mile

The great Victorian historian and novelist, J. A. Froude, rented two houses on the land between North and South Sands in Salcombe for many years — first, The Moult, and later Woodville, now called Woodcot. In 1879, Alfred Tennyson broke a yachting holiday along the south-west coast to stay with Froude at Salcombe. He left the yacht on a glorious evening in early summer. It was Sunday and the sound of church bells carried clearly over the water as the yacht sailed down Salcombe harbour, across the sandy bar, where the waves swished and turned, and out to sea. Tennyson carried the impressions of the evening in his head for some months, until they bore fruit in one of his best-known poems, *Crossing the Bar*.

When walking on this path, natural cliff erosion takes place and the walker should at all times follow the 'acorn' signs even if they differ slightly from the following description.

From the National Trust car park at Sharpitor, the walk takes the lane down to the road, following the way signposted to Courtenay Walk and Bolt Head. The walk turns sharp right down the lovely tree-lined Courtenay Walk signposted 'to Bolt Head' with the acorn sign of the long distance path. There are splendid views through the woodland on the left to the sea and estuary below. Soon the downhill path comes to a white signpost indicating that the road ends here and the way beyond is a public footpath. The walk follows this clearly marked path, climbing quite steeply uphill now. After having negotiated a large kissing gate on the path, and passed several seats, the walk comes to the lower side of Sharp Tor where the railed viewpoints are reached by stone steps and then passed. From here, the views down to sandy Starehole Bay and of the jagged, rocky coastline are magnificent, with the Mewstone and Bolt Head showing on the far side of the bay. The sands of Starehole Bay are the graveyard of a Finnish four-masted barque, the *Herzogin Cecilie*, which struck the Ham Stone, west round the coast, in 1936 and foundered in the bay.

The walk now descends the cliff side of Sharp Tor, still following the clearly marked coast path, round to Bolt Head, crossing a stone slab bridge over a stream which flows into the sea below Sharp Tor. From here, the path, close to the cliff edge, is very steep, but the views are marvellous and make the climb well worthwhile. Once the top of the 420-foot Bolt Head is neared the path becomes much easier, with plenty of grass to relax on. Do not venture onto the old coastguard observation buildings as they are unsafe and to do so could cause a disaster.

Just over half a mile from Bolt Head, the walk reaches Off Cove and The Warren, and carries on over a stile in a wall which reaches out to the path from the right, ignore the right-hand turn at this point but continue up the hill and over the next stile in a similar wall. Beyond we depart from the coast path (and the acorn signs) and turn sharp right and follow the clear path with the wall on your right. At the end of the long field which this wall protects, on the other side will be found a stile giving access to the derelict farm buildings of Middle Soar. Pass the buildings on your left, ignoring all crossing tracks, and go through the gate into the next field. Choose the track that carries half-right up the centre of the field to come out on a farm lane. Here, the walk turns left, arriving almost at once at a National Trust car park on the right. A signpost 'To Coast' directs you over to the left-hand corner of the car park and past a sign saying 'East Soar' and onto their access drive which takes you past a coastguard station, fenced off on the left, towards the cliffs.

After about half a mile, the path curves to the right, and the walk, passing a Youth Hostel sign, stays on the path to East Soar Farm. At the farm the path keeps to the left of the main buildings and negotiates a stile on the left-hand side. Once over this, the path keeps to the right-hand edge of the field, going through a gate just before the far corner, to continue downhill to a junction of paths. Ignoring the stile and gate on the right, the walk turns left to follow a clear path through bracken and gorse and out on to another field where the path turns half-right, downhill, to negotiate a stile and stone bridge to come on to a broader path.

Once on the broad track, the walk turns left in the direction of the sea and Sharp Tor. After about three-quarters of a mile, the walk reaches the crest of the 406-foot Sharp Tor, where the viewpoint indicator and seascapes and landward horizon could hold your attention for some little time.

From here, the walk continues on the path to the left, with fenced farmland on the left and the Salcombe estuary to be seen on the right, ignoring all side paths to various view points, which can be explored if the whim takes you. After about a quarter of a mile beyond here, the path passes an Ordnance Survey triangulation point, and then drops down towards Sharpitor, passes over a stile and through a clump of trees, descending with the help of stone steps to a right turn into a rocky tree-filled gulley. About a quarter of a mile beyond here, the path leads the walk back into the car park for Overbeck Gardens at Sharpitor.

A Coast and Country Walk from Westward Ho!

Pusehill — Abbotsham

MAP:	Ordnance Survey 'Landranger' sheet 180; 'Pathfinder' No. 1254 (SS 42/52).
DISTANCE:	About 4 miles.
ROUGH GUIDE TO TIME TAKEN:	2¼ hours.
TERRAIN:	Easy hill, road and cliff-path walking.
FOOD AND DRINK:	Nothing on the route of the walk; several cafés etc. in Westward Ho!
TRANSPORT:	Pay and Display car park in Westward Ho!
FACILITIES:	Toilets opposite public car park.
START AND FINISH:	Car park (as above). Grid reference 431292.

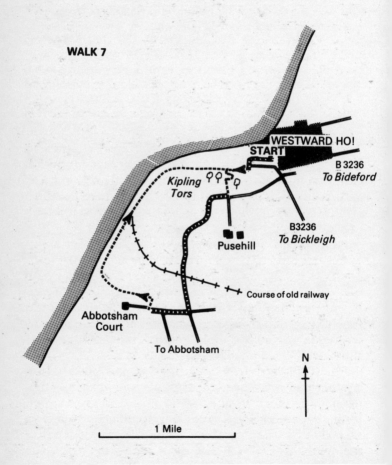

WALK 7

WESTWARD HO!

START

B 3236
To Bideford

*Kipling
Tors*

B3236
To Bickleigh

Pusehill

Course of old railway

Abbotsham
Court

To Abbotsham

N

1 Mile

Despite the fact that this walk takes its name from the great novel of Elizabethan adventure written by Charles Kingsley in the mid-nineteenth century, its closest literary connection is with that great writer of Empire tales, Rudyard Kipling.

The building of the seaside resort of Westward Ho!, set on the tip of land north of Bideford, the town in which Kingsley wrote Westward Ho! in 1854-5, was begun in 1863, its planners no doubt confident that calling the resort after one of the most popular novels of the day would be to its advantage.

Rudyard Kipling's connection with Westward Ho! stems from the fact that he was educated in the United Services College there from 1878 to 1882. For 30 years the college occupied a terrace of 12 Victorian houses, now called Kipling Terrace, in the town near the coast path, along which Kipling used to walk with his school friends. He was to use his school experiences, including his coast path walks, as material for his schooldays' novel, *Stalky and Co.*

This walk's starting point is the main car park in Westward Ho! Coming out of the park, turn left uphill and then right along the road; the road then swings left and uphill slightly to join Atlantic Way where you turn right to come to a sharp left-hand turn in the road where Merley Road joins.

From Merley Road continue up the B3236 for about 50 yards to a sharp left-hand bend where a footpath starts on the right. The walk keeps to this path, ignoring a path off to the right to a holiday centre. After 50 yards the path narrows and is lined with brambles. Already the walk is high enough up to offer good views across the holiday camp and up the three mile length of the famous Pebble Ridge and Westward Ho!'s flat, safe beach.

About 200 yards from the road, there is a junction with another path from the left, and this walk takes the left-hand way, which is quite steep now and zig-zags up through the woods. Log steps in the path help make it an easy, though sharp climb, which soon comes out above the tree tops so that the views along the coast are extensive.

Soon, the path meets other paths at a 'cross roads', our walk takes the left-turning path which goes uphill towards a familiarly-shaped National Trust sign with its back to us, indicating that the land here is part of the Kipling Tors. A steepish walk along this path brings one through a gateway and out on to a surfaced road.

Ignoring the road to Pusehill, straight ahead downhill, the walk turns right. The road, which is reasonably wide and set between banks and hedges — though walkers will need to keep well into the side to allow traffic to pass — takes up the middle section of this walk and offers splendid views over the north Devon hill farm country. At first the road, which has few houses on it, goes gently uphill, then curves round to the left and then starts running gently downhill. The downhill tendency continues for rather less than a mile until it reaches the bottom of the valley it is crossing. About 50 yards before the line of trees stretching across the road, the line of the old Bideford to Westward Ho! railway can just be made out. From here, the road heads uphill again for about a third-of-a-mile until it reaches a T-junction.

Here the walk turns right (ignoring the left-hand turning signposted 'Abbotsham'), and continues along the tarmacked road for another third of a mile (ignoring a second left-hand turning signposted 'Abbotsham') until it ends at a gate into Abbotsham Court.

The walk now turns right to follow the signposted public footpath which runs along a surfaced access road for about 150 yards to a stile on the left. The footpath sign directs the walk over the stile and on to the rolling tor and downland above Abbotsham Cliff.

Although the path becomes indistinct after 100 yards or so, the way is easy and follows the left-hand side of the field to another stile. Again the same direction is taken for a 100 yards or so where another finger-post points diagonally down across the field to a third stile in the corner, on the other side of which is the Somerset and

North Devon Coast Path. Turning to the right on this, the walk now follows the path back to Westward Ho!, 1½ miles away.

At this Abbotsham point on the coast, the path is almost down to the level of the rock strewn shore-line, but once the site of the old Cornborough firing range is reached, the path has begun to climb up from sea-level and is soon high enough to offer good views along the coast in both directions.

Due to erosion of the cliffs, the coast path varies from time to time and the 'acorn' path signs should be followed. Soon the path turns inland slightly to go between the embankments of former railway cuttings, coming abruptly round a corner of the cliffs on to the greensward below Kipling Tors. Following the path below the Tors, a path is soon seen to the right up some log steps. Take this path back towards Westward Ho!, above the old railway track.

Above the first few chalets another National Trust sign for Kipling Tors is seen but the path continues below this and above the roof-tops soon to return to where you went up the log steps near the beginning of the walk. Retrace your steps back the way you came to the car park.

On the trail of Tarka the Otter

Great Torrington — Weare Giffard

MAP:	Ordnance Survey 'Landranger' sheet 180; 'Pathfinder' Nos. 1254 (SS 42/52) & 1274 (SS 41/51).
DISTANCE:	About 6½ miles.
ROUGH GUIDE TO TIME TAKEN:	3½ — 4 hours.
TERRAIN:	Moderately easy railway line and country road walking, about one-third of it hilly. NOTE: This part of the Tarka Trail will not be officially opened to the public until the end of 1992. People walking it before this date do so at their own risk.
FOOD AND DRINK:	Puffing Billy restaurant at Rothern Bridge in the former railway station building; Cyder Presse Inn at Weare Giffard (bar meals, pleasant terrace overlooking River Torridge.
TRANSPORT:	Free public car park on western outskirts of Great Torrington, on A386.
FACILITIES:	Toilets in public car park.
START AND FINISH:	Public car park and picnic spot above River Torridge. Grid reference 485194.

WALK 8

River Torridge

To Bideford
A386

ANNERY
KILN

A386

Weare Giffard Hall

N

WEARE
GIFFARD

Beam Mansion

*Beam
Weir*

Golf
Course

A386

Railway Station

Rothern Bridge

START

A386
To Torrington

Disused
railway

1 Mile

Henry Williamson's enchanting and moving story *Tarka the Otter* has been a favourite with children and adults alike since it was published in 1927. Set mostly in that part of North Devon watered by the Torridge and Taw rivers, the story tells of the life and dramatic death of an otter and of his relationship with the other wild creatures of the rivers' countryside and with Man, his constant hunter.

The early part of this walk, from Rothern Bridge to Weare Giffard Cross on the A386, is over a 2½-mile section of the now disused railway line which first reached Great Torrington from Bideford in 1872. For most of the way the railway track is within sight or sound of the river which, on this stretch, flows northwards towards the Taw-Torridge estuary in a series of loops. For those acquainted with Henry Williamson's story, this is a particularly interesting section of the Torridge, for many incidents in Tarka's action-packed life, from his birth to his death, took place along it.

The walk starts by walking down the hill on the right-hand side of the A386 road on the wide verge to cross Rothern Bridge. From the platform of the disused station at Rothern Bridge on the A386, step down on to the track bed to set off in the direction of Landcross and Bideford (that is, from the left-hand end of the platform as you face the track and keeping to the left-hand side).

Short stretches of the track are set between embankments, but for most of the way the views across the flat fields on either side of the Torridge, rising up to the hills beyond the far bank, are extremely attractive and are marked by farm buildings, a large house or two, and the villages of Weare Giffard and Annery Kiln.

The line crosses the river, high up on iron railed bridges, three times along this stretch. Just beyond Beam Weir, where Tarka and his sisters played, and where the wide weir and its sluice gate can be clearly seen from the railway bridge above, the railway also passes under a high arched bridge which takes traffic from the nearby A386 into Beam Mansion, now an Adventure Centre, and which also figured in the Tarka story.

By the time the railway line nears Weare Giffard Cross, the track crosses a bridge over a road sandwiched between the main A386 and the track. Immediately after the bridge is a gate onto this road, which is taken, the route doubling back under the railway line and, after 300 yards or so, crossing the Torridge once more, this time over a picturesque hump-backed bridge.

The next three miles of this walk are along this narrow, tarmacked road which winds its way along the eastern edge of the Torridge flat-lands (which are liable to flooding, so that there is no regular path along the river itself) and on the hills above.

Passing through the pretty little village of Annery Kiln, the walk keeps to the road signposted Weare Giffard, climbing uphill past houses and between quite high, hedge-lined banks until Weare Giffard's Holy Trinity Church is reached, set up above the road on the right and and with a line of grave-stones peering over the churchyard wall rather like a set of teeth. Past the church and the walled grounds of Weare Giffard Hall, the road curves left back on to the flat land bordering the river, offering a footpath on its left-hand side to take walkers into Weare Giffard village, just two miles from where the walk joined the road from the railway line at Weare Giffard Cross.

Through Weare Giffard, the walk keeps to the main road, now signposted to Torrington, and ignores the road on the left to Gammaton.

Beyond Weare Giffard the road climbs uphill between hedges and embankments again. After about a mile of gradual climbing , the fairways of Great Torrington Golf Course come into sight on the right and it is here, just past the entrance gate to the golf course, that the walk leaves the road to take a clearly marked turning to the right on to an unpaved track wide enough for cars.

The track, which has viewing seats dotted along it, curves round to the left past two of the golf course's greens. The path is high up here offering fine views of the river and hill and farm country around Great Torrington, the bracken and gorse-covered land dropping towards the A386 and Rothern Bridge.

The path continues down, through the bracken, with the tantalising sight of the car park on top of the hill on the other side of the valley. After reaching the bottom, the path soon climbs up again towards the car park.

Around the Arlington Estate

Ferny Park — Smallacombe Bridge — Barton

MAP:	Ordnance Survey 'Landranger' sheet 180; 'Pathfinder' Nos. 1214 (SS 64/74) and 1234 (SS 63/73); National Trust leaflet No. 13, Arlington.
DISTANCE:	About 5½ miles.
ROUGH GUIDE TO TIME TAKEN:	3 – 3½ hours.
TERRAIN:	Woodland and hilly farmland, with short distance of narrow and steep country roads.
FOOD AND DRINK:	Restaurant at Arlington Court.
TRANSPORT:	Free National Trust car park opposite main entrance to Arlington Court (signposted off A39 north of Barnstaple.) Non-National Trust members must pay to enter the grounds of Arlington Court.
FACILITIES:	Toilets available in grounds.
START AND FINISH:	The front of Arlington Court. Grid reference 612406.

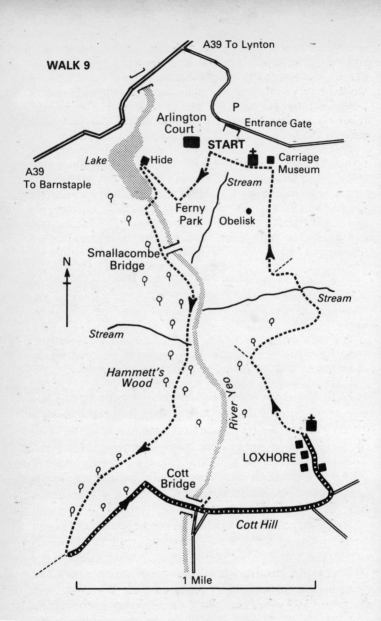

WALK 9

A39 To Lynton

P Entrance Gate

Arlington Court

START

Lake   Hide

Carriage Museum

A39 To Barnstaple

Stream

Ferny Park

Obelisk

N

Smallacombe Bridge

Stream

Stream

Hammett's Wood

River Yeo

Cott Bridge

LOXHORE

Cott Hill

1 Mile

62

Arlington Court, near Barnstaple in North Devon, is a particularly attractive National Trust property, once the estate of the Chichesters, a prominent family among North Devon's landed gentry. Although the estate came into the Chichester's possession by marriage in the 14th century, the present relatively modest Neo-Georgian style house was built only early in the 19th century, replacing an older residence.

The house, gardens and grounds have been carefully restored since they were left to the Trust by the last Chichester owner, Miss Rosalie Chichester, in 1949. To visit Arlington is to step back into a quieter, more assured age than our own, for the house offers a splendid view of English domestic life among the Victorian country gentry. Outside, gardens, a park and farmland complete the estate, much of which was planted with woods and stands of rhododendrons and other plants to provide cover for game birds. Miss Rosalie Chichester, disapproving of shooting, turned much of the park into an animal sanctuary, and the descendants of her Jacob's Sheep, Shetland ponies and other creatures may be seen here today.

The walk explores the southern section of the Arlington estate, taking in both parkland and farmland and making use of the paths and tracks laid out by the National Trust.

Having come out of Arlington Court by the front door (the main entrance) you should walk half-right along a grassy track and find a stile and gate in the corner of a fence separating the garden from a section of the park. The walk crosses the stile and follows a clearly marked path, from which you see Jacob's Sheep grazing, Shetland ponies and, after about 80 yards, a large beech tree, its trunk lichen covered.

The path continues across the park on a broad grassy track now in Ferny Park, heading slightly downhill towards the River Yeo, sometimes crossing stiles on the route finally coming down on some narrow wooden steps onto a crossing stony surfaced path. You turn right for about 100 yards and cross a stile and continue along the shingly track, with rhododendrons prominent on

63

either side, to reach one of the garden's carriage drives. Ahead is a hide from which you may observe the bird life on the L-shaped lake (created in the mid-19th century by damming the River Yeo).

From the hide, you should return to the carriage drive and then turn right to follow the lakeside path. The stone urn on a plinth which you will soon see on the right on a grassy clearing sloping down to the lake is a memorial to Miss Rosalie Chichester.

When the walk, now following the line of Monkey Puzzle trees, reaches the south-east end of the lake, it turns right to cross the dam and then left to follow the River Yeo downstream through a lovely wooded landscape.

Soon the track divides with one arm turning left to cross Smallacombe Bridge over the river, but our walk continues along the broad track (once a carriageway) by the river, following it as it curves round and passing on the left Tucker's Bridge over the river. Soon the track, having crossed a tiny stream, climbs up into Hammett's Wood, passing through several gates, some of which are netted. Close them carefully, then turn right through another gate and immediately left. Follow the waymark signs and a hard climb brings you up to another stile to emerge into an open field with views over the Yeo Valley to Loxhore. In late autumn this is a riot of colour. Keep to the top side of the field with the ancient hedge on your right to pass over another stile in to the dense wood of Cott Down plantation.

The walk follows the track through the woodland until it comes to a very narrow, high, vertical ladder-stile — the locked gate at the side will have to be scaled by those who are not sylph-like — where it comes out onto an unsurfaced and stony country lane, which is part of the southern boundary of the Arlington estate. At the road, the walk turns left to follow the road along the ridge of the hill, turning right to come downhill over Cott Bridge over the River Yeo and so on to the Barnstaple Road.

The walk keeps left here, passing an Arlington estate gate, with the Chichester heraldic herons on top of the posts; continuing on this road, you walk up steep Cott Hill towards Loxhore noting the ancient road sign fixed to the wall of the last farm on the right. In the summer months this hill may be by-passed by going through the gates and rejoining the main path later with a more gentle climb. The route, however, climbs the narrow road, sunk between high banks topped with hedges, so some care is needed, in summer particularly.

After half a mile, the walk comes to a narrow left turn signposted Loxhore Church, and turns down here to pass between the houses and farm buildings of Loxhore. Where the road curves to the right to end by the church lich-gate, a prominent bridleway sign points to a gated, grassy lane off to the left between hedges and contours around above the River Yeo. Where the path emerges onto an open field continue straight across into the woodland opposite where there are now Blue (bridleway) waymark signs. Follow these signs through Deerpark Wood where, part-way through, those people who have opted for the less hilly route rejoin the path. In general, you always keep to the path that is above and follows the stream that can be heard babbling along below. There are many tiny streams flowing down across the path making it muddy in wet weather, but eventually the path turns left, crosses the main stream and, after passing through a gate, emerges into open fields.

This is the East Park of Arlington estate, and is not open to the public, so walkers must remain on the path, being careful to shut all gates encountered on the way. You should keep to the path which turns left out of the woodland, ignoring the Yellow Waymark sign directing people over the stile in front of you towards Barton Courts, but turning left, then right after 50 yards or so between stately trees. Here you can see on your left the obelisk erected to mark the site of a great Jubilee bonfire in 1887. Eventually, after passing through a small wood, the path comes to some farm buildings. Now, the bridleway turns left then along a surfaced lane. Do not continue far along this lane as you need to turn left just short of the cupola-topped stables (housing the carriage museum) and follow the track which soon becomes the carriage drive back to the house. However, if you miss this turning, on your left you will find a lane which will take you past the church to a gate back onto the same drive.

Around Grimspound, an early Bronze Age Village

Grims Lake – Broad Barrow – Bennett's Cross

MAP:	Ordnance Survey 'Landranger' Sheet 191; 'Pathfinder' Nos. 1313 (SX 69/79) & 1328 (SX 68/78).
DISTANCE:	About 7 miles.
ROUGH GUIDE TO TIME TAKEN:	4 hours.
TERRAIN:	Moderately easy walking over open moorland, though with steep sections. In misty weather the walk should be done only by experienced map and compass users. Further, not all of the route is on Public Footpaths but entire area is Open Access.
FOOD AND DRINK:	Best to take your own; the Warren House Inn is a short detour from the last section of the walk, however.
TRANSPORT:	From the eastern direction on B3212 take road signed 'Widecombe' continue over crest of hill and park on roadside just before the right-hand bend.
FACILITIES:	Apart from the inn there are no toilets on the walk.
START AND FINISH:	Opposite car parking. Grid reference 698808.

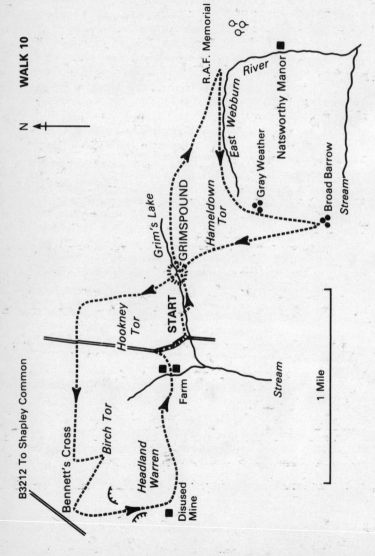

WALK 10

N

R.A.F. Memorial

East Webburn River

Natsworthy Manor

Gray Weather

Broad Barrow

Stream

Grim's Lake

GRIMSPOUND

Hameldown Tor

Hookney Tor

START

B3212 To Shapley Common

Bennett's Cross

Birch Tor

Headland Warren

Farm

Stream

Disused Mine

1 Mile

The sight of Grimspound, the best-known of the Bronze Age pounds, or walled enclosures, on Dartmoor, brings pre-history and the Beaker People (so-called because of the shape of the pottery they made) very much alive for the many hundreds of people who walk it every year.

Grimspound is a sizable village enclosed within a great wall 9 feet thick and 6 feet high. Inside are 24 small, granite-walled hut circles, which would have been covered with turf or thatched roofs. Some of the huts had protected entrance passages, and archaeologists have found signs of human habitation, including charcoal from fires, in about half of them.

There are still gateways on the south, east and west sides. The southern one is a great gateway, built of dry stone masonry. Since the site looks indefensible, it was probably built by pastoral people not as a defence against enemies but to protect their sheep and cattle from wild animals, and would have been occupied any time between 2000 and 700 BC, and perhaps into the early Iron Age, c. 450 — 250 BC.

The walk starts by climbing the steps on the roadside opposite the car park to reach a path which, crossing Grims Lake — a stream, not a lake in the recognised sense of the word — after a short distance, brings the walker to the great circle of Grimspound. The stream, Grims Lake, is liable to dry up in hot weather and runs right through the settlement. The views from up here are splendid.

After admiring Grimspound, continue through the gateway of the compound on the far side and along the path. This path gradually climbs up for a short distance and then bears right slightly with another, smaller path branching off to the left. Keep to this path and after a quarter of a mile or so, just before the path begins to descend steeply, will be seen a granite finger of rock sticking up on your right, make for this along a broad grassy track.

This pointed stone is a memorial to the crew of an RAF

bomber which crashed here in 1941, as the faint inscription notes, and it was erected at the request of the mother of one of the four crewmen killed.

Now there is another broad grassy track almost parallel with the one you have been following, turn right along this path and continue with it for about half a mile, following it round a fairly sharp left-hand turn. As the path climbs gradually upwards, a large barrow will be seen on top of the hill slightly to your right. This is Broad Barrow and the stone on top of it states the fact and, on the other side, has the letters 'DS' on it.

All the barrows hereabouts carry the mark of the mid-19th century Duke of Somerset who once owned the land; look for his initials on marker and boundary stones on the journey.

Turn sharp right on to the broad track towards Hambledon Tor and you are now on the Two Moors Way which we will continue with until Bennett's Cross.

The Two Moors Way is a long distance route from Ivybridge, south of Dartmoor, to Lynton in the north of Exmoor. The original concept came into being in 1965 and it was agreed by all concerned that it was a very good idea although difficulties were raised by the farming community in 1970. Eventually all the problems were solved and the path was opened on 29 May 1976. Many people have enjoyed the walk, which is 103 miles long, because of its unique peace and quiet and avoidance of all large communities.

From Broad Barrow, a Bronze Age burial mound, the broad path on the Hambledon Ridge passes the remains of Hambledon Cross on the left then on to Hambledon Tor, which has an Ordnance Survey triangulation pillar on its summit.

This is a splendid viewpoint, offering great vistas over much of North Devon, as far as Exmoor in the north-east, and the country to the east as far as the Blackdown Hills in the far east of Devon and the start of Somerset.

From the Tor descend steeply down to Grimspound, entering it by the large south gateway and walk straight across it, cross the boundary wall on the north side, then Grims Lake and climb up to the top of Hookney Tor. After admiring the view to the north whilst getting your breath back, carry on across the top and take the path straight ahead to a stone wall which you pass through and turn left down by the side of a stone wall to the Shapley Common – Widecombe road near the crest of the hill that you came over to park the car. (If, as is very easily done here, you came down by an earlier path to the road, turn right and walk up the hill to the stone wall on your right. Similarly, if you came down further over then turn left to the stone wall).

The walk now crosses the road to a path which travels over a slight rise through heather and bracken, to a crossing grassy path, then up more steeply to breast the ridge on the northern side of Birch Tor, where you can see the B3212 road winding along the bottom of the hill and into the distance. For those who are more energetic, there is a path on your left which will take you up to the top of Birch Tor which is clearly visible. Whether or not you take this path, there is a clear route down to the car park below with Bennett's Cross near its northern side.

If you wish to visit Warren House Inn which is a good place for food and drink, another diversion is now possible along the road for half a mile. After which it is possible to rejoin the walk by crossing the road in front of the Inn and walking down to where the paths meet, as mentioned later.

The walk now circles the car park and takes the path diagonally down and across the hump seen in front. This is the start of some old mine workings and paths abound in the area going in all directions. Take the ones that appear to be the most suitable and eventually you will come down to a little valley with a stream at the bottom.

Continue along this path until a crossing of paths is apparent, this is near an old building and the power cable poles which march up the hillside from out of the valley. Those that have refreshed themselves at the Inn, rejoin us here.

The walk veers left along the main track, following at first the line of poles, then the wall of the old mine workings with old broom trees growing at the side of the path. The path climbs steadily up towards the saddle between Birch Tor and Challacombe Down but always on the Birch Tor side. Eventually the top is reached and you can look down and across the valley to where your car is parked. The path continues round and down Headland Warren towards Headland Warren Farm. Go past the farm on the left-hand side and climb up to the Shapley Common – Widecombe road again. At which, you turn right to your car.

Dartmouth Castle

Blackstone Point — Warren Point — Little Dartmouth

The walk takes in a section of the South Devon Coast Path and part of the English Heritage's property around Dartmouth, offering superb views of coast, sea and countryside.

MAP:	Ordnance Survey 'Landranger' sheet 202; 'Pathfinder' No. 1358 (SX 85/95).
DISTANCE:	About 3¼ miles.
ROUGH GUIDE TO TIME TAKEN:	1½ — 2 hours.
TERRAIN:	Well marked cliff path, rocky in parts and gentle hilly track inland from coast.
FOOD AND DRINK:	Teashop at Dartmouth castle, open most days in summer.
TRANSPORT:	Free public car parking (signed) on side of road above Dartmouth Castle, limited parking at Dartmouth Castle. (Walk may be started near Little Dartmouth, in which case parking is at the free National Trust car park there, reached by taking the B3205 from the estuary road and turning right at Redlap Cross on to Redlap Road; the car park is sign-posted.)
FACILITIES:	Toilets are close to the car park at Dartmouth Castle.
START AND FINISH:	English Heritage car park at Dartmouth Castle or the turning point in the road above Dartmouth Castle if parked in this road. Grid reference 886504.

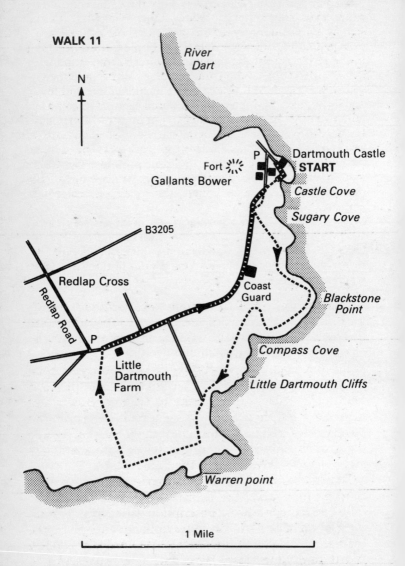

WALK 11

N

River Dart

Fort
Gallants Bower

P

Dartmouth Castle
START

Castle Cove

Sugary Cove

B3205

Redlap Cross

Redlap Road

Coast Guard

Blackstone Point

P

Little
Dartmouth
Farm

Compass Cove

Little Dartmouth Cliffs

Warren point

1 Mile

Dartmouth Castle, the object of this walk, has guarded the narrowest part of the Dart estuary since the 15th century. The ruins of its contemporary fellow guard, Kingswear Castle, stand on a promontory on the opposite shore of the Dart.

Dartmouth Castle was originally a simple fortification built in the 1380s against the raiders and pirates from Brittany — this being the time of the Hundred Year's War — and there is still sufficient left of the later castle, including a round tower and its ramparts, complete with restored cannon, to give a fair indication of the site's strategic importance. Dartmouth Castle, which may be visited at the start or finish of this walk, is reached from the English Heritage car parks by walking downhill a short way to enter the castle grounds. The Castle and St Petrock's Church within the precincts are open daily throughout the year, though the castle is closed at Christmas.

Note, too, in the car park area, the path to the right to Gallants Bower, once a Civil War redoubt and now an English Heritage owned pretty woodland area, with good bird life, rising to 400 feet (120m) above the mouth of the River Dart: worth a detour.

To start the walk from the entrance to Dartmouth Castle, look for the path that climbs to the left of the ruins. Take this path as it meanders upwards to emerge at a gate in an iron railed fence immediately opposite the car turning point of a road. (Those who parked on the upper road join at this point). There are several paths and the road here. Ignore the path opposite to Gallants Bower and turn sharp left; here you will see a path descending to Sugary Cove and one gently climbing up the hill beside the road signed with the Long Distance Path acorn sign and a yellow arrow. This is the path to take.

Due to erosion of the cliffs, the coast path varies from time to time and the 'acorn' path signs should be followed if the following description varies from that on the ground. The path continues uphill to emerge on the road at a path sign and Compass Cottage. At this point take the almost level lane, signed with the usual acorn, to your left. This is surfaced for a short distance until it passes the last of the cliff-top houses here when it becomes stony. The path is within the Trust's Little Dartmouth property, which extends for one and a half miles along the cliffs west of the mouth of the Dart.

To the left, the land drops sharply down to the sea, and both Dartmouth and Kingswear Castles may be glimpsed through the trees, brambles and bracken which clothe the hillside. Soon some painted aerial and flag masts come into view in front of you just before the path suddenly turns left and then descends almost to sea level. As the path curves round to the right, you are on Blackstone Point.

In stormy weather the spray and crashing surf is deafening as the sea rushes into the rocky gullies, even in a quiet time the surf makes a fierce noise on the rugged rocks. Do not try to descend into these gullies as they are very dangerous due to the wet and slippery nature of the rocks. Having rounded Blackstone Point, where a gun battery was placed in the 17th century, you cross a footbridge over one of the larger narrow gullies with caves cutting into the right-hand cliffs. Once over the footbridge, stay on the right-hand path to reach Compass Cove, about half a mile from the start of the walk; from here, one of the first submarine cables was laid beneath the Channel to Guernsey in 1860.

From Compass Cove, the walk climbs up inland and away from the beach. Look for a stile in the right-hand fence, waymarked with an acorn. (Ignore the path that carries on and into the cove.) Having crossed the stile you follow the path uphill until you are well above the cove, with bracken and gorse on either side, to reach a signpost, ignoring all side paths as these are mainly sheep tracks. This is a strenuous climb and you may well pause to get your breath back so that you can enjoy the view. Soon the white-painted coastguard buildings rise on the hill to the right, above. Eventually an acorn on the sign directs you to turn left and the climb is much more moderate. The path is high up here and the views are extensive as you approach the stile on the crest of the climb.

The path now passes round Willow Cove and a stile and footbridge have to be negotiated. Later, after the route has passed through an old gateway in a wall, it cuts across Warren Point, from where on clear days the views of Start Bay and Start Point are good. There is a plaque on Warren Point marking the contribution of the Devon Federation of Women's Institutes which helped the Trust to buy the Little Dartmouth Cliffs.

Beyond Warren Point, the path stays with the cliff until it suddenly turns inland, to your right, and passes through several stiles towards Little Dartmouth Farm, a field away to the right. The final stile brings you into the National Trust car park and onto the road; here you turn right to pass between Little Dartmouth Farm and Willow Cottage to reach the lane which takes the walk east over the spine of the hills, with farmland on either side, and back to Dartmouth Castle car parks, passing the coastguard houses on the right and Compass Cottage on the left, enjoying the extensive views over the estuary.

Hayes Barton
and Sir Walter Raleigh

East Budleigh Common — Bicton Common
—Yettington — Hayes Wood

MAP:	Ordnance Survey 'Landranger' sheet 192; 'Pathfinder' No. 1330 (SY 08/18).
DISTANCE:	About 3½ miles.
ROUGH GUIDE TO TIME TAKEN:	2 hours.
TERRAIN:	Woodland and hilly moorland, fairly steep in places with a short distance of country road.
FOOD AND DRINK:	Sir Walter Raleigh Inn and Grasshopper's (tea, coffee, snacks) in East Budleigh; cream teas are occasionally available at Hayes Barton in the summer months.
TRANSPORT:	Large free car park in woods on East Budleigh Common Road.
FACILITIES:	No toilets available on the walk.
START AND FINISH:	Car park (as above). Grid reference 042848.

WALK 12

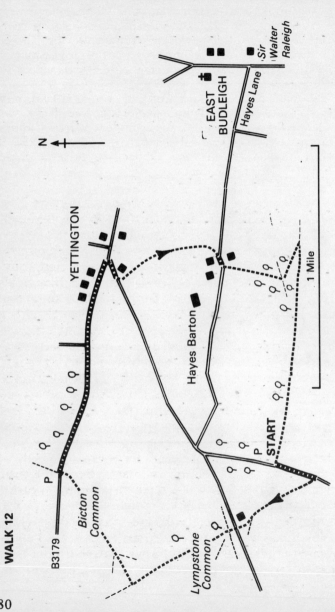

EAST BUDLEIGH

Sir Walter Raleigh

Hayes Lane

YETTINGTON

Hayes Barton

B3179

Bicton Common

Lympstone Common

START

P

1 Mile

N

Sir Walter Raleigh, the Elizabethan explorer and literary gentleman, was born at Hayes Barton, a Tudor farmhouse west of East Budleigh, in 1552. The house, a pleasant thatched and gabled building, is still there. Now a private dwelling, it is not open to the public, though the owner, who does the occasional bed-and-breakfast in the season, may also offer cream teas in the summer.

Beyond Hayes Barton lies wood and common land, very popular with walkers and picnic-parties in fine weather — and with the Marines from the nearby Lympstone Barracks, whom you may well encounter emerging, covered in camouflage, from various copses and covers, although they usually exercise outside the summer months.

To reach the starting point of the walk, drive to East Budleigh, which lies off the A376 north of Budleigh Salterton. From the centre of the village, turn on to Hayes Lane which goes off the main street, High Street, directly opposite the Walter Raleigh Inn; the lane is signposted 'to the birth-place of Sir Walter Raleigh'. You drive along this typically sunken, narrow Devon road for about one and a half miles, passing Hayes Barton on the right after a mile, to a T-junction. Here, you turn left and left again after 50 yards or so, to come on to a slightly wider road through woodland. There are numerous parking places, with notices asking people to observe the Country Code etc., off both sides of the road, but you should keep driving for rather less than a quarter of a mile until you come to a markedly larger parking area on the left (if you have left the trees on the right, you have gone too far). Here you park the car to begin the walk.

Since walkers and riders have tramped paths of their own through the bracken here, there is a maze of paths, seemingly designed to confuse anyone trying to follow a more precisely described walk. However, the description below is based on the more obvious paths and so long as you keep walking in the direction stated, you should not get lost. In the unlikely occasion that you do, you will eventually emerge at a metalled road and can stop someone and ask the way to Yettington to resume the walk.

From the car park, the walk turns left along the road for rather less than 400 yards, before the next clump of woodland on your right. Here you should then see a reasonably wide path (about a yard), gravelled at this point and clearly defined, going off into the bracken. Our walk follows this path up through the bracken and passing gorse clumps until, at the top of the rise, it meets with another wide path at a small grassy area. Here, the walk turns right on to this bridle path, to reach very soon another car park with a brick built abandoned garage near the metalled road. (If you do not emerge at a car park or if it does not have an abandoned garage, it is probably because you missed the grassy patch and the right turn at the top of the rise; if so you will have come out on to the Lympstone Common road a hundred yards or so too far west, and you should turn right and walk along the road until you come to the car park with the abandoned garage).

From this car park, the walk crosses the tarmacked road, down a short piece of rough track, to yet another car park. Exiting from this car park, in line with the entrance track, is a wide track — sometimes with a wooden barrier across it to prevent unauthorised vehicles going along it — which you follow for about 400 yards. At the start of some gravel workings another broad path goes off to the right, which you follow downhill through a small copse of Scotch pines (they are the ones with the long needles!) to a junction of three other such broad paths. As you came down the hill, you would have seen a path going up the hill in front of you, this you now make for over a rather marshy area. You climb the hill and, whilst recovering your breath, admire the view before continuing. Again you see across the next little valley, but slightly to your left, another path meandering up the other side. Again you make for this path which climbs steeply up to the top of the hill to emerge on to another broad track. You turn left here and then almost immediately right to arrive at the B3179 road at Bicton Common.

Here the walk turns right and follows this road, which runs unfenced and mostly downhill for approximately a mile to the village of Yettington. Just before the main part of the village is reached, you will see a signpost on the right-hand side of the road, stating 'Exmouth 4½ miles'. Here, you turn right, over a metal-railed bridge across a small stream. On the left, about 70 yards beyond the bridge just past a farm building, the walk comes to a stile by a gate, with a 'Public Footpath' sign pointing across it. The walk now follows this path across fields, and around the hill which rises behind Hayes Barton, to come down on to the road from East Budleigh by the farm buildings of Hayes Barton. Hayes Barton itself may be seen by walking up the road a little way and then returning to the point at which you joined it.

Cross the road and take the path immediately opposite, up a driveway past Hayeswood Cottage and into the woods to turn first right and then left by the footpath signs. As you climb up through the woods, the path divides and you take the lower right-hand path which, although it still climbs up the hill, is sunken until it comes out at a crossing of paths. Ignoring the two side paths and taking the one directly in front, you come down to a broad track. At this green lane, you turn sharp right and follow it through the woods and out onto the heath and moorland again, gently climbing all the time. Ignore all the interesting side paths and keep in the same general direction and you will, after about half a mile, suddenly come out into the car park where you left your car.

The Iron Duke

Culm Davy — Culmstock Beacon
— Wellington Monument

MAP:	Ordnance Survey 'Landranger' sheet 181; 'Pathfinder' No. 1277 (ST 01/11).
DISTANCE:	About 7 miles.
ROUGH GUIDE TO TIME TAKEN:	3½ – 4 hours.
TERRAIN:	Partly woodland, pastureland and open heath with some road walking, hilly in places.
FOOD AND DRINK:	None available on the route — best take your own picnic.
TRANSPORT:	Free car park at Wellington Monument.
FACILITIES:	No toilets available on the walk.
START AND FINISH:	Car park (as above). Grid reference 145167.

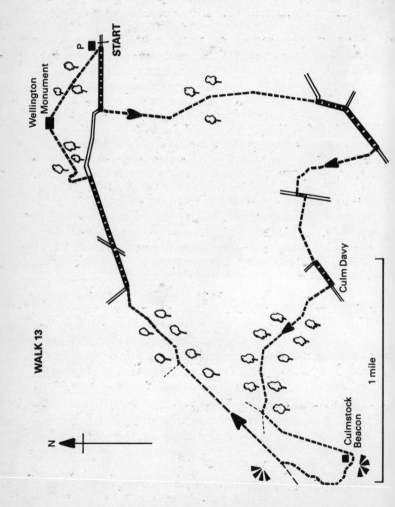

WALK 13

N

START

P

Wellington
Monument

Culm Davy

Culmstock
Beacon

1 mile

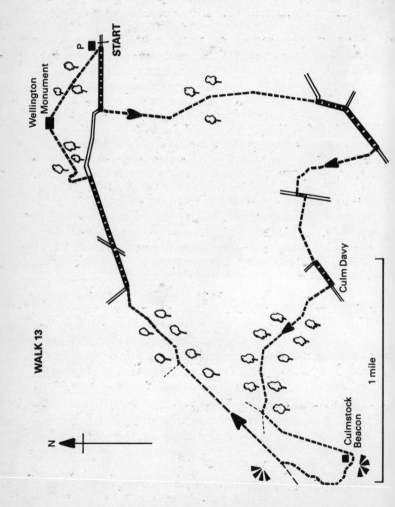

86

The Duke of Wellington acquired the name Iron Duke after his exploits in the Battle of Waterloo. Born Arthur Wellesley, a member of a long-standing Irish family, he bought part of the Blackdown Hills above Wellington town in the early 19th century when he became Viscount Wellington of Wellington after distinguishing himself in the Spanish Peninsula War. He was created Duke of Wellington after further successes in the wars. Following the Duke's victory at Waterloo, the local gentry decided to erect an obelisk in his honour on the highest part of the hill thereabouts which turned out to be on the Duke's own land. It was started in 1817 but was left incomplete until the death of the Iron Duke in 1852. The monument was eventually completed in 1892 — 75 years after the start of the project.

In 1933, the trustees of the monument gave it and the surrounding 17½ acres to the National Trust for the enjoyment of the general public.

Initially there were to be many cannon installed on the site but when they arrived at Exeter Quay they were found not to be the type used at Waterloo and they were left there. Some time later four cannon were installed at the monument site but during World War II they were taken away for scrap, an act of vandalism in the extreme. It was reported that they were never melted down and many people endeavoured to find them, without success. Later, during restoration work at Exeter Quay, three cannon were found and one was presented to the National Trust for installation at the monument site, and is still there.

This walk starts from the monument car park near the road and turns right along the road for 400 yards when a sharp bend in the road is reached, at this point a stile is found in the left hedge by a gate. The way is over the stile, the first of several, while the path follows an almost straight line, initially over pastureland then through low scrub, into woodland and pastureland again, all the time views are opening up to the left down the Culm valley, eventually to emerge after a mile at a metalled road on the top of a steep hill.

From the top of the hill, the walk carries straight down

the road to the T-junction where you again turn right and continue down until a farm, Culm Pyne Barton, is reached; immediately opposite is a large tree with a brook flowing under it and, to the left a farm gate with a public footpath sign. Take this path along the top edge of the field, then across the centre of the next to arrive at a typical Devonian sunken lane where we turn left to some farm buildings. These we follow around to enter another field and start to climb up the left side to a metalled road. The walk now turns left and immediately past the farm on the right we are confronted by two gates into their farmyard, take the right one and up into the field behind the yard, a gap in the hedge is seen to the right which we go through and up this next field with the hedge on our left. At the end of the hedge is seen a stile giving access to the cottage (there may be a wire in front for stock control but this is easily straddled).

As you pass this cottage and up its driveway, please note its beautiful aspect and state of preservation — it is a great credit to its owners with the thatched roof and typical cottage garden. You have now arrived at another metalled road and a sharp bend. Carry on forward for about 150 yards where the road turns sharp left and disappears downhill into Culm Davy. Here turn right up a lane which shortly passes a cottage on the right, then a steep climb into woodland. At the next junction of paths take the left track on so that you continue in the same line as before with the hill falling away to your left and climbing to your right. You pass another cottage, seemingly miles from anywhere and you wonder how the people in this beautifully preserved cottage manage with none of the amenities that we take for granted. The path still climbs uphill through the woods suddenly to turn right and come out on to open heathland — you are now on Blackdown Common.

You turn left now, along the top edge of the wood and, once past it you start getting the outstanding views to the south with, as you continue, Hemyock nestling down in the valley behind you near the eastern end of the Culm valley. All too soon you reach Culmstock Beacon — a little round house on the end of Blackdown Common overlooking Culmstock way below you. Some say that this was a sobering up prison for the drunkards of Culmstock — if it ever was, who brought them up here? As we turn right now, the western end of the Culm valley comes into view and in one place you can see way down to Uffculme and beyond. The famous racing stables of Martin Pipe can be seen below and to your right at Nicholashayne. The path now slowly descends to come, after some 300 yards, to a crossing track which we take to the right. Initially you get the views now to the west over towards Exmoor and the Brendon Hills before the path takes you across the heath towards the radio mast. Eventually you pass it on your right as you start a short but steep descent to the metalled road. Continue along this road past the cross roads, and after about 300 yards or so you will see a muddy track on your left with a bridleway sign. Take this track for 100 yards to a gate on your right into woodland, once through the gate turn right again, almost parallel to the way you came, along a narrow path that climbs, slowly at first, then as it turns left, much more steeply to go along beside a wall on the right. You continue along this path until the Wellington Monument comes into sight.

You pass a plaque, which describes the monument and its history, to the cannon where another plaque tells you of all the views you can see, even over to the Welsh Coast. On some days, especially in the summer holidays, the entrance is open for the very energetic to climb the many hundred steps to the three spyholes at the top of the monument. Continuing away from the monument along the broad track, you soon reach your parked car and the end of the walk.

Beautiful Blackdowns

Kentisbeare — Blackborough

MAP:	Ordnance Survey 'Landranger' sheet 192; 'Pathfinder' No. 1296 (ST 00/10).
DISTANCE:	About 7 miles.
ROUGH GUIDE TO TIME TAKEN:	3½ hours.
TERRAIN:	Easy walking at first on lanes and pasture fields but increasing in steepness towards half way, then through woods, narrow lanes and tracks.
FOOD AND DRINK:	The Wyndham Arms, Kentisbeare
TRANSPORT:	Park under the wall outside Kentisbeare Church.
FACILITIES:	No toilets en route, except in Wyndham Arms at the management's discretion.
START AND FINISH:	Kentisbeare. Grid reference 064082.

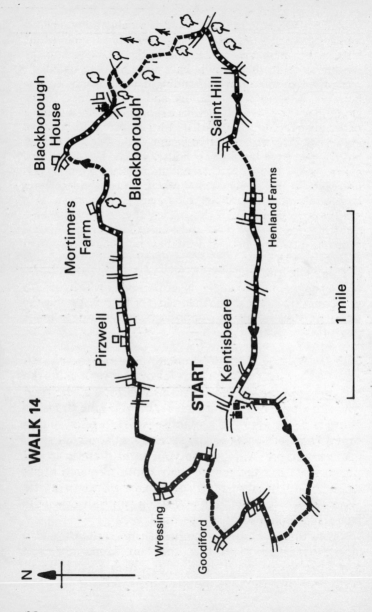

WALK 14

N

Blackborough House

Mortimers Farm

Blackborough

Pirzwell

Saint Hill

Henland Farms

START

Kentisbeare

Wressing

Goodiford

1 mile

92

Kentisbeare, where this walk starts, is a mile off the A373, the Cullompton to Honiton Road, and is a delightfully mellow-looking place in a beautiful setting. Nestling in a fold of the hills in the Culm Valley, it is one of the gateways into the Blackdown Hills. These hills have now become nationally recognised as an area of outstanding natural beauty. Kentisbeare itself is steeped in history and is mentioned in the Domesday Book. As well as a village shop, post office and inn it has many interesting houses. The 15th century church has an ancient rood screen reputed to be one of the finest in Devon. Nearby is the medieval priest house, which has its original oaken screen, buttery hatches and an unglazed window. It is not open to the public. Many of the houses and cottages hereabouts are constructed of Devon cobb, which is a sandstone construction on the inside and outside with a lime mortar between stones and rubble infilling. The whole is rendered on the outside. Many of these buildings have bowed walls caused by damp seeping through the thatch at one time and weakening the walls. Much more of the history of the area can be sought from either the village post office which carries a number of small books on the locality, or from inspecting the tapestry in the reading room opposite after enquiring from the post office.

Start by walking through the gate between the church and The Wyndham Arms and follow the path round to the right to emerge almost opposite a fork in the road with a signpost saying Dulford. Taking this lane you soon come to a gate after the last house with a bridleway sign on it. This path leads across several fields to come to a gate into an old lane. Just to your right there is an old pond now not much more than a muddy patch but it used to hide the smugglers' contraband ('Brandy for the Parson, Baccy for the Clerk'). We then continue down the lane to the main Kentisbeare road.

Cross this road and continue in the same direction across three fields to reach another lane. Here, turn right and walk up to the T-juction, at which turn left and continue down the road ignoring the road coming from the right. The road slopes gently down to find, at the end of the field on the right, another gate and footpath sign. Take this and follow the clear waymark arrows beside a leat to the fisheries on your left, cross the stile carefully because there is quite a drop on the other side and walk across the stream. This is the overflow for the leat and there is never much water in it. Now cross the next large field half left to the stile, where you turn right along the bottom edge of the field to emerge at a narrow lane. Here turn left and up to a small settlement with a barn on your right. Turn right up the narrow lane beside.

After some half a mile you come to another road which you cross and go down the continuation of the lane to come out at another little lane. Turn left here and then right after a short distance; soon you are walking through the little hamlet of Pirzwell and up a narrow country lane to cross yet another lane. This lane goes up and down and you can see the little village of Blackborough nestling under the hill up ahead.

Continue up, then down this lane which suddenly turns left and after half a mile you find Mortimers' Farm. The track now continues on the right of the farm, through a small wood and out to a stile beside a gate. Cross this and go straight ahead to come out into a field. You cross this diagonally to the left and carry on up the sunken track which, at one time, was one of the driveways to Blackborough House. You emerge through a gate onto Blackborough House Lane with Blackborough House on the left.

Blackborough House is a shell of its former glory. It was built about 150 years ago by the late Lord Egremont as his family seat. It is not one but two houses — one for himself and the other for the incumbent of Blackborough Church. Unfortunately, Lord Egremont ran out of money and died before the house was fully completed. The house fell into disuse for some time and then was taken over by the Quakers who removed all the ornamentation, including the fine marble staircase. The house then became variously a farm, hospital, hostel and probably many other things as well before the present owners, who are carrying out restoration work, took it over.

With Blackborough House behind, now turn right and up the hill to Blackborough Church after passing the beacon on the right.

All Saints Church, Blackborough, celebrated its 150th birthday in 1989. It was also built by Lord Egremont and, as you enter the church, you will see a framed print of it on your left. This shows how the church was supposed to look when it was first built. The spire was originally stone but this proved too heavy for the tower and was soon replaced by a much shorter, wooden spire with wooden shingles. The tower houses a single bell which can be heard from a great distance over the valley below. You notice when you enter the church that it has two balconies, where the two main families of the area sat — the Perseys and the Wyatts. The Earl's pew is blocked off, but is above your head as you enter. The church is very cold in winter and originally the only form of heating was two fire places one in the Earl's pew and the other in the vestry. You might like to try to discover where on the outside the chimneys are. An old anecdote goes that when the Earl got tired of the sermon he used to rattle his poker in the fireplace.

To continue with the walk from the church gate, half left is a path from a hunting gate and a stile. This path climbs the hill steeply to emerge at a crossing of paths. Turn left here and after a hundred yards come to a sharp bend with one of the best views in Devon over the Culm and Exe Valleys to Dartmoor and beyond. On a clear day, with binoculars, you can see the Merrivale radio mast some 50 miles away.

The path then continues to a junction of paths where you turn left and can look forward to a level or downhill walk all the way back. At the end of the broad track turn left through a gate and emerge at a road. Cross this and a few yards further on to the left will be seen a gate into the woods, go through this and hard left to walk down a narrow path leading down through the woods to a junction of five paths. Go straight across them and take the downhill track almost opposite (the others either go uphill or are level).

With views across to Dartmoor and Exmoor, continue down this lane, at first rather stony then it gradually improves as you approach the first houses in Higher Sainthill. Suddenly the lane descends rather rapidly before bending to the right and left to come out by the Baptist Chapel. Here turn left along a narrow lane to come out into a field by a gate. Cross this field to the gate that is by a stream down in the depression in front of you. Here bear half right and along a grassy lane to come to the little hamlet of Higher Henland which was owned by Alfred the Great. Continue down and then up past Lower Henland to the concrete road which extends down to a tarmacked road.

Cross this road and turn left for a few steps before turning right down an overgrown green lane. Initially it looks rather daunting but with perseverance it is walkable. This lane continues down between fields with an unimaginable amount of wildlife in it. Eventually it becomes less overgrown and is a wide lane to emerge at another tarmacked road, at which go straight ahead to arrive in Kentisbeare.

The Drewe Arms, Broadhembury

Broadhembury — North Hill

MAP:	Ordnance Survey 'Landranger' sheet 192; 'Pathfinder' No. 1296 (ST 00/10).
DISTANCE:	Just over 5 miles.
ROUGH GUIDE TO TIME TAKEN:	About 2½ hours.
TERRAIN:	A pasture and woodland walk with the first part on a road, sometimes steep as the walk climbs away from the valley.
FOOD AND DRINK:	The Drewe Arms at normal opening hours.
TRANSPORT:	Car parking round the square in the village of Broadhembury. The village is clearly marked from the A373, which is the Honiton to Cullompton Road.
FACILITIES:	Toilets in the Drewe Arms at the management's discretion.
START AND FINISH:	Broadhembury Village. Grid reference 101048.

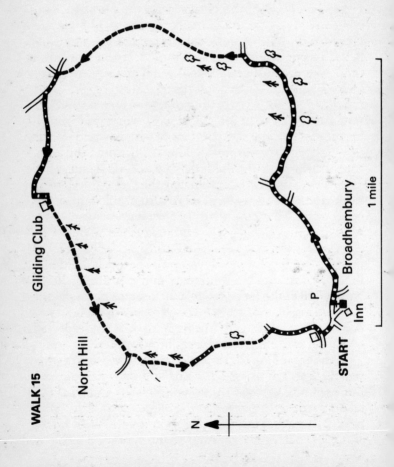

WALK 15

North Hill

Gliding Club

START

Inn

Broadhembury

P

N

1 mile

Broadhembury is a picture-postcard village with hardly a house which is not thatched. This is because the Drewe family, who own the major part of the village, insist that the character of the village is maintained. You will not see a television aerial in the village because these too must be hidden away. The church and the inn — The Drewe Arms, of course — are well worth a visit, even if it is only to refresh yourself before the arduous climb.

From the centre of the village, with the post office and village shop on your left, walk up the road — signed Dunkeswell. Take no notice of any right or left hand lanes or roads, but continue along this road. It now gently rises then goes down slightly. Then gradually it starts a long and steep climb for the best part of 1¼ miles — it seems much longer but it is usually a quiet country lane without much traffic. Eventually the road flattens out but just before that you will see a bridleway sign on your left. Take this path with the woods on your left to come through a gate and drop down the little vale and up again on the other side. First this is a green lane then onto the edge of a field with a gate at the end. Here turn sharp right and up to the road where you turn left.

After about 50 yards, the entrance to the Gliding Club can be seen on your left. Walk up this road to emerge through a gate after which you turn sharp left and follow the road through the buildings and out along the left hand edge of the field. DON'T be tempted to walk onto the field itself — it can be dangerous when gliders are taking off or landing. A towing hook is heavy especially when descending from several hundred feet.

At the end of the Glider Field you will find a gate with a steeply descending path. It is not far down this stony path but keep a sharp look out to your left for a narrow path leading further down on the level portion of this stony path. However, you may like to enjoy the view further along, in which case continue on the path until it rises up onto the edge of the North Hill. The views here are extensive over the Otter and Culm Valleys and, on a clear day, into Dartmoor.

Returning back, just before the track rises steeply, you should be able to make out a faint track leading half right and steeply downwards through the gorse, brambles and bracken. Soon this gives way to fir trees and suddenly you come to a track which leads down to a gate at the entrance to a field marked with the yellow waymark arrow. If you do not see it at first, it is probable that you will have to walk a little to your left at the bottom edge of the trees.

When facing the gate (if it is there, as sometimes it seems to vanish mysteriously only to re-appear a few weeks later!) walk straight across the field keeping in a generally downhill direction to find a stile into some woods. Go through these woods and emerge into another field, where in the bottom left-hand corner is another stile. Climb over this and along a short wooded track to emerge into a much larger field where you continue downhill and over the last stile into a lane. This lane leads down to the village again over a little humpbacked bridge with a ford beside (many people paddle in the stream to cool off on a hot summer's day) and you return to your car.

The Rock Inn, Haytor Vale

Haytor Down — Bag Tor — Lewthorn Cross —Smallacombe

MAP:	Ordnance Survey 'Landranger' sheet 191; 'Pathfinder' No. 1341 (**SX** 76,77)
DISTANCE:	About 5 miles (a shortened version, reducing the walk by 1 mile, is suggested).
ROUGH GUIDE TO TIME TAKEN:	2¾ hours for the full walk.
TERRAIN:	Moorland walking with some steep sections; country lanes and roads for a quarter of the distance.
FOOD AND DRINK:	Rock Inn; during the tourist season there are mobile ice-cream and snack vans in the various car parks.
TRANSPORT:	Free car park on road below Haytor.
FACILITIES:	Toilets adjacent to car park.
START AND FINISH:	Car park (as above). Grid reference 765773.

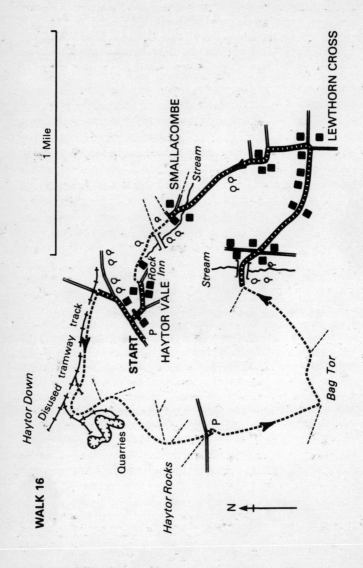

WALK 16

1 Mile

Haytor Down

Disused tramway track

Quarries

Haytor Rocks

P

N

Bag Tor

START

HAYTOR VALE

P

Rock Inn

SMALLACOMBE

Stream

Stream

LEWTHORN CROSS

Haytor Vale is a pleasant moorland village above Ashburton and Bovey Tracey. The Rock Inn there is an old, family-run establishment offering accommodation, imaginative snacks and bar meal menus at a stylish comfortable bar, and restaurant meals, seven days a week. It is a free house and serves real ale. Outside there is a most attractive garden for fine days. However, parking is limited nearby.

Near the car park entrance there is a Dartmoor National Park notice board which gives a brief history of the area and is well worth reading before starting. Continuing right along the road past the Moorlands Hotel and Craft Centre and the road to Haytor Vale there is, after a little distance, a minor road bearing off to the left. Take this for about 50 yards to a standing stone at the point where the old Holwell and Haytor quarry tramway crosses the road. Turn left on to the tramway and follow the course of the granite 'rails' up the moor.

This tramway was opened by George Templar, in 1820, to transport the granite from the disused Holwell and Haytor quarries down to the waiting boats on the Teign at Teigngrace. They once provided the stone for many London landmarks including the old London Bridge (now in America) and the British Museum. Unfortunately the quarries had a short life from 1820 to 1860 because the relatively cheap Cornish granite forced the closure of them. The name of the mine owner still lives on with the recent creation of the Templar's Way, a walk of some 15 miles from Holwell quarry down to the river below at Teigngrace. You will notice how the granite slabs have been shaped to guide the wheels of the horse-drawn wagons; the wheels were flat and the 'rails' were flanged, unlike modern railway practice where the rails are flat and the wheels are flanged.

After about half a mile you come to a junction to the left. (Note the hole in the granite 'rail' where an iron blade pivoted to guide the wheels in the chosen direction.) Follow the left-hand track in a wide circle across an embankment to the foot of the now disused granite quarries. Where the the tramway turns right into a deep working, the walk keeps straight ahead and skirts the workings to the right, climbing steeply up through the bracken towards Haytor Rocks. The walk passes to the left of the rocks, though you should pause to admire the extensive views in all directions. (A path, for the more agile, is available to climb to the top of the rocks where the panoramic view is even better on a clear day.) Now, you head down the moor towards the road, in the same general direction as before, where the car park on the top of the hill is crossed. The path slightly to the right, crossing the moor somewhat below the top of the ridge, is the one you require.

Once over the brow, the walk heads for Bag Tor, a small pile of rocks in the middle distance, with, in front of it, a wall running from left to right with two gates close together in the middle.

When you arrive at the wall, turn left and follow it until it turns sharply to the right at the corner of the field. At this point a well-trodden path heads straight on, falling gently down the side of a shallow valley, scattered with granite scree. The walk follows this path around the edge of the moor, heading for a row of small houses amongst the trees. After about half a mile the path joins and runs alongside a wall and trees. In the lowest corner of the open moorland is a gate and a footpath signpost. The walk turns right through the gate, and then straight ahead down a steep track into woodland.

You cross the stream at the bottom, then climb steeply up to the road.

For a quick return, you could turn left here and follow the road back up to a cattle grid, where you turn left back to the car park.

To continue the walk, go straight ahead along a fairly main road which, after a short distance, drops away down the south-eastern edge of Dartmoor. After just over half a mile there is a cross-roads — Lewthorn Cross. The walk turns left here and follows a narrow, deep lane steeply downwards. At the foot of the valley, at a road junction, it turns left and then right through a group of houses and when the road turns sharply to the right, keeps straight ahead up the lane to Smallacombe. This old farmhouse and its outbuildings are reached after about a third of a mile; you bear right through the farmyard and then left and across a shallow ford. Shortly afterwards, the track turns to the right with a three-way signpost at the junction, but you should keep straight on to Haytor Vale, along a footpath which climbs up through a most picturesque wooded valley, with a little stream gurgling through the undergrowth on the left. After a while, the path crosses a wooden bridge and then, almost immediately, up a ladder-stile before turning right and resuming the upward trend with the stream now on your right. A little further on the stream passes underneath once more in a pipe. At this point ignore all paths to the left and right but continue on up the valley, shortly to pass, on your left, a short branch of the stream issuing from a cave at the foot of sheer sides of a rocky cliff.

The path continues upwards, crosses the stream once more, and finally, as the gradient eases, the left fork is taken through an old kissing-gate-type stile (there is no gate as such), then right at the top of the path on to a rough lane to bring you out on to the road just a few yards above the Rock Inn and Haytor post office.

From the Rock Inn, the route travels up hill on the road to reach a T-junction where the right-hand turn is taken to lead, across a cattle grid, onto Haytor Down again. The wall on the left is then followed to return to the car park where you started.

The Castle Inn, Lydford

White Lady Waterfall — Devil's Cauldron

MAP:	Ordnance Survey 'Landranger' sheet 201; 'Pathfinder' No. 1327 (SX 48/58).
DISTANCE:	About 3¼ miles.
ROUGH GUIDE TO TIME TAKEN:	1¾–2 hours.
TERRAIN:	Clearly defined path, much of it through forest, often steep and slippery. Do NOT wear open-toed shoes or sandals but sturdy walking shoes or boots with a good grip. NO dogs allowed. Not accessible for push-chairs. Non-members of the National Trust have to pay an entrance fee.
FOOD AND DRINK:	Castle Inn; café in Lydford; tea-rooms at main National Trust entrance and above White Lady Waterfall at Manor Farm.
TRANSPORT:	Free car park in Lydford opposite the Castle Inn.
FACILITIES:	Toilets adjacent to car park, at National Trust entrance and at Manor Farm.
START AND FINISH:	Car park (as above). Grid reference 510849.

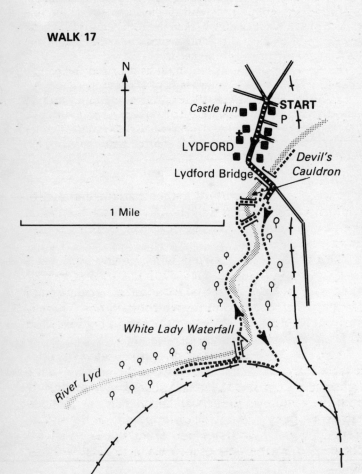

WALK 17

N

Castle Inn

START

P

LYDFORD

Devil's
Cauldron

Lydford Bridge

1 Mile

White Lady Waterfall

River Lyd

Disused railway

108

Lydford is a small village to the north-west edge of Dartmoor, reached via a turning off the A386 north of Tavistock. Though its greatest claim to renown comes from its nearness to the famous Lydford Gorge, it is of some interest in its own right since it dates back to Saxon times, when it had a mint, and can still show the remains of a great earth rampart thrown up as part of defences against marauding Danes. Lydford also has, in a picturesque group at the end of the main street, the fine church of St Petrock, dating back to the 13th century, the great square keep of the castle, and a pleasant painted inn, the Castle, set to the right of the keep.

The castle keep was, in fact, built as a prison for people offending against the stannary laws of Dartmoor.

Lydford Gorge is National Trust property and may only be visited through the two National Trust entrances and during its opening hours — 10.30 a.m. to 6 p.m. daily April to October (short sections from the waterfall and the main entrance are open daily November to March).

This walk begins at Lydford, rather than the entrance to Lydford Gorge, so that walkers may also see the castle, the church and the dizzying view over Lydford Bridge down into the Gorge.

The Castle Inn, the starting point for the walk, dates back to Tudor times, though today it has an attractive air of Charles Dickens' 19th century about it. It offers good meal and snack menus in its two-roomed bar. There is likely to be a bright log fire in the bar in cold weather while its garden is pleasant in summer.

From the Castle Inn's front door, the walk turns right to walk along the main road towards the gorge. On the right, the walk passes the great square keep, apparently built on a mound, though archaeologists say that the earth was piled up round the castle after it was built. (The castle is open most times but if not the key may be obtained from the post office during normal working hours).

Past the castle is the church of St Petrock, with an

avenue of clipped yews up to it. The church, part of it 15th century, has a late Victorian north aisle and some notable 20th-century carving and choir screen. Outside near the south door is an amusing epitaph on the tomb of George Routleigh, a local watchmaker. Opposite to the Church is a memorial stone erected in 1990 to commemorate the Battle of Lynden Ford in the year 997.

Beyond the castle and church, the walk keeps to the main road, which curves round to the left to reach after 250 yards or so Lydford bridge, from where one may obtain a first glimpse of the gorge. Here, upstream of the Pixies' Glen, the gorge is a steep, deep ravine, quite gloomy with bushes, trees and plants; in this section is the appropriately named Devil's Cauldron (look downstream over the right-hand parapet of the bridge). Underneath the bridge you may see how the Lyd riverbed has been 'potholed' by boulders, brought downstream by the fast-flowing river and swirled round and round so that they gouge out holes in the Upper Devonian slates from which the gorge is formed.

Just across the bridge on the right is the main entrance to the gorge, with a large car and coach park, shop and other facilities. The National Trust request that visitors walk round Lydford Gorge in a clockwise direction because the paths, though well cared for with good footbridges and fencing where necessary, are narrow and often difficult, and may become overcrowded in summer. The Trust has available a clear leaflet map of the gorge.

Much of the walk is through woodland along or just above the Lyd; in some places, the cliff-like sides of the gorge tower above one's head, in others the lovely woods seem alive with the sounds of birds. There are numerous falls and rapids in the river, including the impressive White Lady Waterfall, and a disused railway line to be crossed at its southern end. This is the section of the gorge which, the guide books tell you, is the best example of 'river capture' in Devon. It was caused by the River Lyd, which once flowed down the valley now occupied by the River Burn, cutting back from the waterfall during the Ice Age and breaking into the much steeper valley down which it flows to the Tamar.

The clockwise walk round the gorge takes one downstream above the north-east side of the gorge, turning westwards past the waterfall to take either the longer and easily-sloped path which circles through Westford Wood or a much shorter but also steeper path which zig-zags above the waterfall. Both paths bring one down to the north-west bank of the river to walk upstream to the start of Pixie Glen.

Here, the walker has the choice of either crossing the river to return to the picnic area or of carrying on along the north-west bank and visiting the Devil's Cauldron from the inside. A short diversion to it can get crowded in the summer months and, as the notices state, you can have as much as an hour's wait to see it. It is also not suitable for those who are not sure-footed or animals. The final section of the walk has a path on one side of the river only, so the walker must return the way he came to get back to the main entrance. From here, the return to Lydford is back over Lydford Bridge and along the road into the village.

The Peter Tavy Inn

Harragrove — Merrivale — Godsworthy

MAP:	Ordnance Survey 'Landranger' sheet 191; 'Pathfinder' No. 1340 (SX 47/57).
DISTANCE:	About 6 miles.
ROUGH GUIDE TO TIME TAKEN:	3–4 hours (not including the stop at Peter Tavy Inn mid-way through the walk).
TERRAIN:	Footpaths and bridleways over open bracken and heather-covered moorland. Some quite steep hill walking, but mostly not too difficult. Short distances on sunken lanes.
FOOD AND DRINK:	Peter Tavy Inn; Merrivale Inn and Dartmoor Inn, both near Merrivale on the B3357.
TRANSPORT:	Large, free car park on the south side of the B3357, 1 mile west of Merrivale.
FACILITIES:	Toilets are in earlier lay-by or in Tavistock.
START AND FINISH:	Car park (as above). Grid reference 530752.

WALK 18

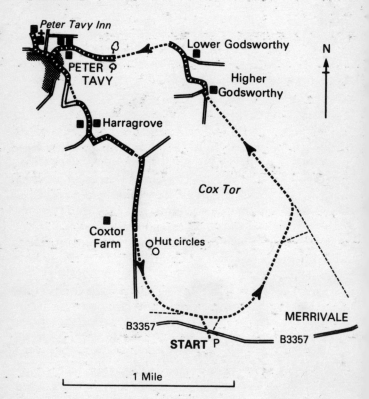

Peter Tavy Inn

PETER TAVY

Lower Godsworthy

Higher Godsworthy

N

Harragrove

Cox Tor

Coxtor Farm

Hut circles

MERRIVALE

B3357

B3357

START P

1 Mile

Peter Tavy is a village of Saxon origin on the western edge of Dartmoor, where the moor has lost its pretty green softness of the south and become much more dour. There are great vistas of grassland with patches of bracken and heather, cropped low by sheep, ponies and the wind, from which jagged tors and rocks rear up to the sky. Some of the farms in Peter Tavy parish date back to Saxon times, and the numerous hut circles, cairns and stone rows indicate Bronze Age habitation.

The four-centuries-old inn at Peter Tavy is the sort of place to which people come in droves at weekends, summer and winter, to enjoy its comfortable, welcoming atmosphere, its real ale and its good bar food. Since children are not welcomed in the bar, it really is a family place only in the summer, when the kids can sit in the garden among the fruit trees.

This circular walk has been planned to make the Peter Tavy Inn a stopping place halfway round.

From the car park, the walk crosses the B3357 to join the broad, grassy path/bridleway which can be seen crossing in front of Cox Tor, and circles round the right-hand (east) slope of the massive tor. After just over three-quarters of a mile, the path is joined by a bridleway that has come up from Merrivale between Middle and Great Staple Tors and then bears left round Cox Tor. The farm buildings below and to your right are Wedlake and to your left belong to Higher Godsworthy Farm, towards which the walk is now heading, reaching a surfaced farm road which continues down to the farm buildings.

Here the walk turns left along a lane walled in on both sides. At the end you turn right and cross a small stream to Lower Godsworthy Farm. The walk then turns left and up a surfaced road for about 300 yards to a stile in the wall on the left hand side. The path then travels down across fields to emerge at a crossing of paths. Take the one labelled Peter Tavy and continue down to a surfaced path and lane to emerge in Peter Tavy at the post office.

The walk follows the road, turning right at the T-junction, then right again at the main village street.

A sign points left down a no-through road, at the end of which, past Harewood Farm, is the Peter Tavy Inn, its stone buildings set round a small courtyard.

After a break at the inn, the walk returns to the main village street, passing the church, *c.* 1500, on the left; this is worth a visit if only to see how badly Victorian 'restorers' could treat an old church.

At the main street, the walk turns right and then left up the road marked by the post office on the corner. Curving to the right, the way is now uphill on a surfaced road between banks and hedges, with the left-hand bank becoming very steep after Broadoaks House is passed, though there is a view back to Peter Tavy over the right-hand bank.

The walk now comes to a gap in the bank on the left-hand side, where stone steps, built into the bank, take you over the stile in the wall and into the field. The path crosses several fields in the general direction of the building on the skyline by means of rather worn stone step stiles to emerge at the surfaced road again. The less sure-footed may prefer to walk along the road. The walk follows this road uphill to Harragrove Farm.

Past the farm, the walk turns left into a lane which, after half a mile, ends at a gate, beyond which is moorland once more. Through the gate, the walk follows the path which runs to the left of a stone wall. Where the wall turns to the right, the walk continues straight on, the path having now become quite wide and grass-covered. At the surfaced farm road which the path soon reaches, the walk turns right onto the road, coming to a high point offering splendid views into West Devon. About 200 yards further along the road, at a point where the walker has the buildings of Coxtor Farm (still a noteworthy example of a typical yeoman's farm of the 17th century) below on the right and the highest point of Cox Tor on the left, a narrow and somewhat indistinct path forks off from the left-hand side of the road, widening out after 180 yards or so to follow the contours of Cox Tor back down to the B3357 and the car park. If you cannot see the path, don't worry just fork off to the left and walk across the heather and bracken towards the car park contouring round Cox Tor.

A viewing table at the western end of the car park, set up by the Royal Town Planning Institute to commemorate its 70th birthday and to 'contribute to the enjoyment of the countryside', identifies the places, hills, tors, etc., seen on the walk down from Peter Tavy. These extend as far as Plymouth Hoe and the sea in the south, and Brent Tor and even Brown Willy in the north-west.

The Royal Oak at Meavy

Yennadon Down — Sheepstor

MAP:	Ordnance Survey 'Landranger' sheets 201 and 202; 'Pathfinder' No. 1349 (SX 46/56).
DISTANCE:	Approximately 4 miles, including detour to Sheepstor.
ROUGH GUIDE TO TIME TAKEN:	2 hours.
TERRAIN:	Moderately easy hilly walk, with a short steep section and some road walking.
FOOD AND DRINK:	The Royal Oak at Meavy. In the summer months a mobile van will be found at Burrator Reservoir selling ice creams etc.
TRANSPORT:	Free car parking near or off Meavy village green.
FACILITIES:	Nearest toilets are in the Royal Oak or in the car park at Yelverton.
START AND FINISH:	The Royal Oak. Grid reference 541672.

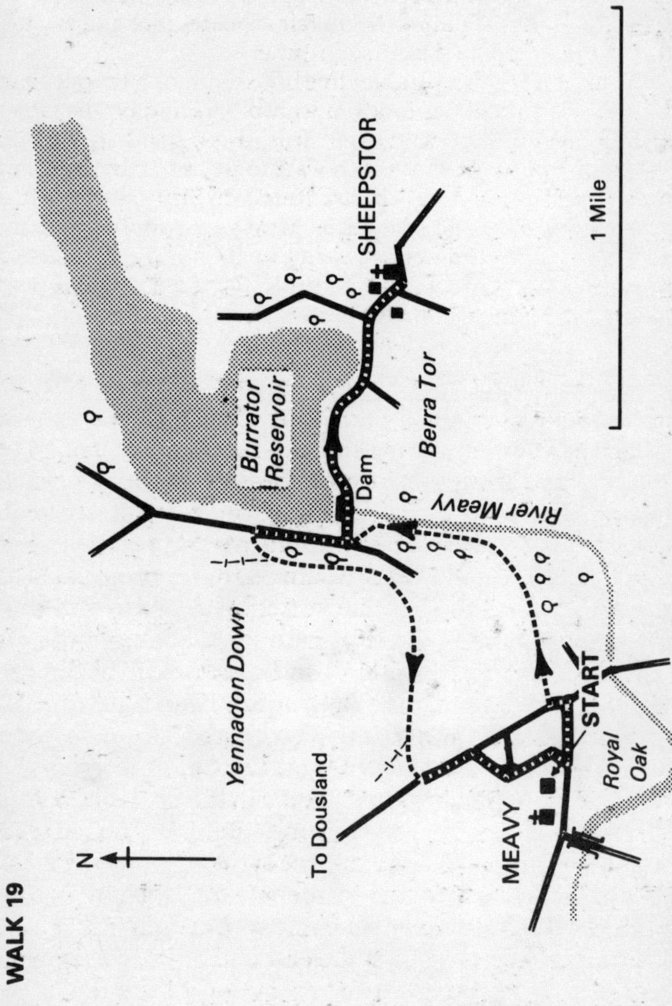

WALK 19

N

Burrator Reservoir

SHEEPSTOR

Dam

Berra Tor

River Meavy

Yennadon Down

To Dousland

MEAVY

START

Royal Oak

1 Mile

Meavy is a pleasant village with a picturesque green on the south-west approaches to Dartmoor. The Royal Oak Inn on the Green, housed in what was once a church house for medieval St Peter's Church, takes its name from an exceedingly ancient oak tree which grows, well propped up, near the inn's front door. Meavy's annual Oak Fair is held under and around the tree on the first Saturday in June.

The Royal Oak is a pleasant free house, offering real ales and a good selection of bar foods in its two bars and on the tables outside overlooking the Green. It is also a good starting-off point for a pleasant after-lunch walk to the attractive Burrator Gorge and the 150-acre Burrator Reservoir. The latter, created in 1898 by damming the River Meavy to supply water for Plymouth, is considered by many to be the most beautiful reservoir lake in Devon; certainly its lovely wood and moorland setting is hard to beat.

From the Royal Oak on the Green, the walk goes east out of Meavy, turning left at the T-junction at the end of the village (Meavy School is on the corner) and crossing the road to go through a gateway beside the house called 'Moor View'. This brings the walk on to a path through woodland, soon crossing the old Meavy Mill leat and following the River Meavy up through the gorge towards the dam, whose high granite wall soon looms up through the trees. On the left a broad path leads back and up to a hairpin bend. At this point can be seen part of the dry channel of Francis Drake's Plymouth Leat, built in 1589 to take drinking water into Plymouth. The path then leads up to the road, where you turn right to cross the dam, perhaps pausing on it to take in the fine view across the reservoir to the tors beyond. Behind you, as you stand on the dam, rises the rocky height of Berra Tor (berra = 'wood', so the name means 'the tor in the wood'), which has given its name to Burrator Reservoir. There is a flight of steps at the east end of the dam giving access to a steep path to the rocky top of the tor.

Sheepstor, one of the loveliest positioned west Dartmoor villages, lies about half a mile from the reservoir. It is well worth making a detour to the village, if only to find the tomb of the Brookes, White Rajahs of Sarawak, in the churchyard.

(It is also possible to walk right round the reservoir, which is about four miles round, but the walk is on a metalled roadway, not a path, and so may not be so enjoyable in summer when traffic is heavy).

Having returned to the dam from Sheepstor, the walk goes back across the dam and turns right to go through a wood glade edging the reservoir. Near a small waterfall on the left, the walk follows the track which turns sharp left to go uphill to what was once Burrator Halt on the old GWR Yelverton-Princetown railway (axed by Dr. Beeching in 1956), accessed by a short flight of stone steps in the embankment near the remains of an iron kissing gate. The view from up here, taking in several tors, including the dramatically sheer Leather Tor to the north, and Sheepstor village, is very good.

The walk now continues along the track of the old railway round the south spur of Yennadon Down. Where the rail track begins to curve round across the down there is a metal gate across and the path turns away to the left of it; the walk now follows the path downhill to cross the dry Plymouth Leat again and then a cattle grid, and so coming to the Dousland-Meavy road. The walk turns left here and goes downhill for 200 yards, where Rectory Lane goes off to the right. The walk goes down Rectory Lane, arriving back in the centre of Meavy on the village green.

The Chichester Arms, Mortehoe

Woolacombe — Morte Point — Bull Point

MAP:	Ordnance Survey 'Landranger' sheet 180; 'Pathfinder' No. 1213 (SS 44/54).
DISTANCE:	About 4¾ miles.
ROUGH GUIDE TO TIME TAKEN:	2¾ hours.
TERRAIN:	Fairly strenuous cliff-top and pastureland walking in Rockham Bay area.
FOOD AND DRINK:	Chichester Arms and several cafés in Mortehoe; numerous eating places in Woolacombe.
TRANSPORT:	Free side-of-the-road parking in Woolacombe on the road above Barricane Beach. If using the main public car park make sure that you have sufficient coins to put into the machine to allow you out.
FACILITIES:	There are several toilets along the front at Woolacombe.
START AND FINISH:	North end of the road above Barricane Beach, Woolacombe. Grid reference 454443.

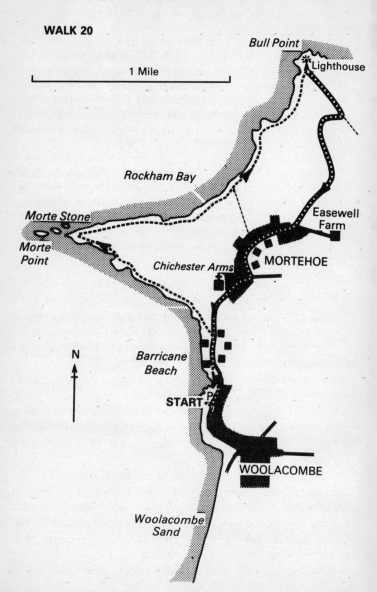

WALK 20

1 Mile

Bull Point

Lighthouse

Rockham Bay

Morte Stone

Easewell Farm

Morte Point

Chichester Arms

MORTEHOE

N

Barricane Beach

START P

WOOLACOMBE

Woolacombe Sand

The Chichester Arms is a pub with a stylish air about it, not least because of the elegant white with blue facings of its paintwork. It stands in the centre of the old village of Mortehoe, on the other side of a tiny square from the interesting Norman church of St Mary Magdalene, which seems to have been little touched since it was enlarged in about 1300. (Many people are attracted to the church by its tomb of one William de Tracey, but historians point out that this is probably the tomb of a rector who died in 1322, and not of *the* William de Tracey who was one of the knights who murdered Thomas à Becket at Canterbury in 1170.)

The Chichester Arms is a good place to aim for as a rest point on a walk on the coast path round Morte Point, a spectacular part of the National Trust's five miles of wonderfully beautiful coastal property between Lee and Woolacombe on the North Devon coast. Not only does the Chichester Arms have an attractive, let's-stay-for-hours bar, but it can also offer a children's room, which is an advantage for families.

Due to coastal erosion the Coast Path may vary slightly from the route described. At all times the Coast Path signs (finger posts or yellow waymark arrows accompanied by an acorn) should be followed. From the coast road above Barricane Beach, the walk heads north (i.e. with the sea to your left) towards Mortehoe. Just where the road curves round to the right a 'coast path' sign points off the road to the left, and the walk follows this path, which has a wooden railing fence on its left side, across a greensward for 100 yards or so (ignoring the steps down to the beach here), to come up to the road into Mortehoe.

The familiar coast path sign now directs the walk to the left along the road between Watersmeet and Haven Hotels. A hundred yards or so on uphill along the road, the coast path leaves the road from the left-hand side (note the signpost) and the walk follows the coast path north-west to round Morte Point.

The coast here is dramatically rocky, given distinctive

shape by the 'Morte Slates' which make up the cliffs and give it razor-sharp edges and shiny surfaces. Waves crash against more reefs of rock reaching out into the sea from the coastal path. As the path reaches Morte Point itself, the infamous reef of rocks which ends in Morte Stone (on which an incredible five ships were wrecked in the winter of 1852) comes into view off the point.

Once round the point the path climbs at first gently and then more steeply to a junction with a short cut path from the south side of Morte Point. From this point the path starts undulating steeply up and down with many steps cut into the rock passing round Rockham Bay. The undulations continue until Bull Point is reached where the lighthouse, built in 1879, now has a particularly powerful fog-horn. (The lighthouse is open, at the keeper's discretion, from 1 o'clock to an hour before dusk).

From the lighthouse, the walk turns to the right off the coast path to follow the surfaced lighthouse access road which leads inland across the rolling green pastureland towards Mortehoe. The path, a service road for the lighthouse, is easy to follow and arrives at a metal gate across the road and then turns right. (At this point there is a narrow path straight ahead, this leads across pastureland and allows access to some hut circles before arriving at Easewell Farm. Then along the drive-way to the road). The main route, however, continues along the access road and arrives at the road into Mortehoe via a kissing gate to the left of a large gate which closes the road to the lighthouse.

The main walk, having negotiated the kissing gate (the entrance to Easewell Farm is on the left here), follows the curve of the road to the right and down into Mortehoe village. This is easy walking down a road with the walls of houses and the hedges of gardens on either side.

This road ends at a T-junction (with the Kingsley Inn on the right and Mortehoe post office on the left). Here, the walk turns right, along a road sign-posted 'Woola-combe'. Soon, the Chichester Arms comes into view, with the church, its churchyard entrance dominated by a lich-gate, a few yards further on down the road. From the Chichester Arms, the walk carries on along this hilly road, which is well supplied with hotels and guest houses, down to the coast and round to the road above Barricane Beach where the walk began.